BEYOND
COMFORT
ZONES

By the time you finally read this
I will have already published the
most gushed over savage Barbie
book the world has ever seen.
Thank you for always believing in
me, I am _so_ excited to work
with you. Just don't laugh
too hard at this book... the
first is always the worst.

Allison.

BEYOND COMFORT ZONES

THE REAL-TALK APPROACH TO DIVERSITY, EQUITY, AND INCLUSION

ALLISON DAVIS

DE&I PITFALLS QUIZ

ASSESS YOUR ORGANIZATION'S APPROACH TO DE&I

Already curious to find out if your company might be experiencing any of the pitfalls discussed in this book regarding its approach to Diversity, Equity, and Inclusion? Gain initial insights by taking the DE&I Pitfalls Quiz.

This interactive quiz is meticulously designed to evaluate your company's current DE&I approach. By answering thought-provoking questions, you'll develop a comprehensive understanding of your organization's strengths and growth opportunities in fostering a truly inclusive workplace that prioritizes equity and attracts and retains diverse talent.

Don't miss out on this opportunity to gain crucial insights and propel your company's DE&I journey forward.

Take the first step towards cultivating a culture that celebrates diversity, nurtures equity, and champions inclusion.

https://www.allisondavis.work/pitfallsquiz

Proceed with caution.

This isn't your run-of-the-mill DE&I book as you might have already guessed due to the lack of DNA strands or captivating colorful symbols on the cover.

I am providing a warning as this book contains unfiltered honesty, potentially uncomfortable revelations, and unpacks complex issues regarding one of the most sensitive and vital topics of our time.

This book dares to challenge conventional conceptions, addresses uncomfortable truths, and shares unexpected perspectives. Brace yourself for a rollercoaster of emotions as we navigate the murky waters of diversity, equity, and inclusion.

Don't brace yourself too much though. Within these pages lies a treasure trove of insights, strategies, and potential solutions that can revolutionize your approach to DE&I. The unconventional approach in this book is simply meant to push your boundaries, and make you question long-held beliefs to prompt transformative growth.

Consider this your invitation to join the ranks of fearless change-makers and disruptors. Together, we'll address tough issues head-on, dismantle old paradigms, and pave the way for a truly inclusive future.

So, if you're ready to dive deep, challenge the status quo, and emerge with a fresh perspective on DE&I, buckle up and be prepared to embark on this unforgettable journey.

Just remember, once you read this book, there's no turning back. Prepare to be enlightened, inspired, and perhaps even a little shocked along the way.

TABLE OF CONTENTS

INTRODUCTION

Corporations have been striving to get diversity right for decades.

Motivation behind efforts have varied, ranging from legal compliance, avoiding the "Netflix special" treatment (looking at you, Abercrombie) to a desire for greater innovation, creativity, and solutions that meet the needs of more diverse customers.

Particularly after the unfortunate incidents that occurred in the summer of 2020, the number of organizations jumping on the DE&I (Diversity, Equity, and Inclusion) bandwagon has skyrocketed.

Companies have responded to the social outrage and intolerance of racism by launching public campaigns and marketing efforts that address movements such as Black Lives Matter or #MeToo.

While the empathy, recognition, and commitment to addressing historical issues is initially appreciated by most, many have lost hope regarding the validity and impact of corporate commitments to Diversity, Equity, or Inclusion.

This is primarily because DE&I efforts have been largely reduced to marketing campaigns that superficially acknowledge real issues, yet ultimately serve to promote the organization's image as diverse and inclusive, shifting the spotlight towards brand loyalty as opposed to any real progress.

The organizations that do put some budget where their mouth is, tend to default to a tired copy and paste approach.

More or less, this is generally the order of operations for addressing and promoting DE&I:

Executives hastily delegate the topic to a single individual or department that becomes accountable and responsible for facilitating immediate change.

Whoever is ultimately held accountable for the outcome of the efforts is usually given a long and fancy title such as Chief of People Officer, Chief Diversity Officer, or Head of Global Diversity and Belonging. Pro tip, the longer and more elaborate the title, the greater the potential for impact.

This individual will often start by quantifying the organization's current diversity and, based on where the organization stands, look to best practices as to what other companies are doing to increase their diversity.

They borrow program ideas or develop their own initiatives on a limited budget, focusing their efforts on quick wins.

They then make an official public commitment to the world by publicizing a report that beautifully displays the quantity of diversity within their current workforce, outlines their future recruitment goals, and announces the initiatives they're planning to incorporate in their corporate strategy.

This report professes to the world their every intention of tracking progress and holding themselves accountable for their representation of women and other underrepresented minorities within the organization.

From a superficial standpoint, these actions appear to be the first positive steps towards progress. After all, they consume a significant chunk of worktime from those involved.

While there is promise in these actions, their ultimate impact remains to be seen.

Because the focus has been primarily on cosmetic changes that only aim to display immediate progress as a reaction to a current challenge rather than getting to the root of the actual organizational issues that block DE&I pertaining to more complex matters such as organizational culture and human behavior, no real progress is ever accomplished.

The generic diversity campaigns, workshops, hiring quotas, and various other initiatives don't end up driving any substantial results, which loses any buy-in from leadership and the rest of the organization that was initially there, leaving everyone in a state of fatigue.

AKA

Individuals who were initially triggered by or uncomfortable with the subject altogether are left even more frustrated by the waste of time, effort, and money.

Current minorities, while they might have been able to navigate the company culture previously, are left in an uncomfortable and potentially even more isolated position.

Additionally, minorities who were attracted and brought into the organization based on the efforts face the assumptions that they were not hired based on their skills or talent but rather because of their status as a minority.

That beautifully written diversity report becomes long forgotten and business carries on as usual until the next social issue or diversity scandal.

This becomes a double-barrel issue:

DE&I efforts are ignored because they don't lead to change.

DE&I efforts don't result in change because management and employees don't have buy in.

Does this sound like a familiar problem in the organization you're part of?

I would be willing to put money down that it is.

While, generally, the widespread acknowledgment of social injustices and attempts to increase the number of minorities that belong to historically oppressed groups within corporate America is a positive thing, through the process, organizations have become so out of touch with what they actually need to be more inclusive, equal, and, therefore, more diverse.

The demand for diversity has undoubtedly gone up as it has become more widely recognized as a crucial factor in achieving long-term business success; however, time, energy, and resources have not increased proportionately.

Therefore, diversity has become this perpetual business problem with no straightforward, actionable solution, which is understandable, as it has more to do with sociology, history, and human behavior, which are a lot less quantifiable and, frankly, can just make people feel uneasy addressing in a professional environment.

The harsh reality is that most companies would prefer a quick fix that helps them prove to the world they're not racist, sexist, homophobic, etc. as opposed to working toward and investing in efforts that contribute to building an environment that allows them to fully utilize their current workforce and organically attract and retain more diversity.

Now, take a deep breath because I'm about to write something you probably don't want to read.

I hate to break it to you, but unfortunately, there's no quick fix for diversity, equity, or inclusion.

If there were, I suppose I would rather be writing about something far more entertaining.

It takes time, energy, and effort to build an authentically diverse workforce. And it takes even longer to be able to realize an entire workforce's full potential.

In this book, I explore the most common pitfalls in corporate diversity efforts and provide actionable insights to help organizations avoid making the same mistakes that prevent them from cultivating a more diverse, equitable, and inclusive working environment.

Through the contents of this book, I hope to bring a sobering perspective in addition to a bit of comedic relief to a sensitive subject. My aim is to facilitate productive conversations and engage a wider audience beyond those who are already passionate about DE&I.

By sharing real-life examples, practical advice, and thought-provoking discussion questions, I hope to help organizations break away from the "copy and paste" approach to diversity. By doing so, organizations will unlock the capacity to truly value and leverage the unique brilliance of every individual, ultimately cultivating an organically diverse workforce.

Whether you embark on this book-reading journey individually or as part of an organizational book club, my intention is to equip you with the insight to identify red flags that indicate your organization is falling into any one of the potential pitfalls I have identified. By fostering critical thinking and encouraging purposeful action, this book aims to guide you towards a more productive, authentic, and effective path.

Now, you might be thinking to yourself "What does this White girl from America know about DE&I?"

I completely understand any skepticism.

However, you will eventually find out that I speak from firsthand experience when it comes to the challenges and shortcomings of corporate diversity, equity, and inclusion.

To make a long story short, towards the end of my time in university, I fell madly in love with a mittelständische Unternehmen, otherwise known as a mid-size corporation in Germany, which proclaimed to value and desire greater diversity. However, through a series of unfortunate experiences as their token employee, I discovered the profound significance of effective DE&I within organizations.

During my time working abroad, the CEO had asked two critical questions that sparked my interest and ultimately led me on a journey to find answers: how can we make current minority employees feel valued within the homogeneous working environment, and what can we do to attract and retain more diverse talent?

Motivated by these questions, I developed an insatiable drive to uncover solutions. My pursuit of knowledge even took me to some of the most extraordinary circumstances in South Africa.

Despite good intentions, I have witnessed companies time and time again fall into the same DE&I pitfalls that prevent them from creating truly equitable and inclusive workplaces.

My collective experience has profoundly shaped my perspective and beliefs regarding the resolution and mitigation of present-day DE&I challenges. While I acknowledge the significance of context and the need for tailored approaches in various environments, my primary objective is to initiate a constructive dialogue and disseminate cross-cultural approaches to DE&I. By doing so, I aspire to assist organizations in sidestepping the common pitfalls I've observed and foster inclusive work environments that value and leverage every individual's unique brilliance.

Regardless of where you are in the world, imagine a workplace where diversity is not a source of distress or panic, but rather a natural part of the company culture; a workplace where all employees feel valued, heard, and supported, regardless of their background or experience; a workplace that attracts top talent from all over and retains employees who are fully engaged, productive, and satisfied.

In such an environment, the possibilities are endless.

Organizations that can leverage the diverse perspectives and skills of all their employees are going to be the ones who come up with unique solutions to complex problems, outperform competitors, and expand into new markets. Not to mention, enjoy the benefits of higher employee engagement, satisfaction, and retention, reducing their turnover and recruitment costs.

Business owners and leaders who can effectively prioritize diversity, equity, and inclusion and focus on leveraging the full potential of all their employees will create a workplace where everyone can thrive, leading to sustained growth and success.

By doing DE&I work the right way, companies have the potential to become audacious innovators in the marketplace, thrive in rapidly changing environments, and achieve extraordinary results.

Reading this book is the first step towards comprehending the common missteps that companies often unknowingly take, that only end up exacerbating their DE&I challenges. More crucially, it will equip you with invaluable insights on how to steer clear of these mistakes and chart your own course towards genuine improvement.

By immersing yourself in the experiences and research shared within these pages, you can evade the costly mistakes that frequently plague companies and instead attain sustainable growth and prosperity.

Don't squander any more precious time, money, and resources on ineffective DE&I initiatives.

It's time to delve deeper, and empower yourself with essential insights and the right mindset necessary to catalyze authentic change and transformation within your organization.

INAUTHENTIC IN DE&I EFFORTS

Is your company going through one of those, oh-shit moments where they realized their award ceremony, corporate brochure or conference panel is entirely composed of White men?

For, like, the fifth year in a row?

Well, fear no more! In all my research, I found the perfect solution to help your organization look not-racist and not-misogynist in no time at all.

In 2016, Arwa Mahdawi developed the website Rent-A-Minority.com to assist companies like yours that require immediate solutions to address their lack of diversity for particularly momentous occasions.

Her platform gives businesses the opportunity to rent minorities from a wide range of underrepresented groups on an as-needed basis.

Immediate options include "The Intellectual Black Guy," "A Smiling Muslim Woman," and individuals who are

"Ethnically Ambiguous" and can check any box that your organization might presently be missing.

Mahdawi describes her revolutionary service as "diversity on demand."

This service is for your organization if they haven't had the time to work on their corporate diversity or if they believe that "actually doing something meaningful to disrupt institutional inequality would be way too much work." (Mahdawi, 2016)

Is this sounding ridiculous to you? I sure hope so.

Obviously, the service was created as a joke; however, over a thousand people signed up to be eligible minorities on the Rent-A-Minority website, and several large companies (left unnamed) reached out, sincerely inquiring about services.

While the absurdity of Mahdawi's experiment might be a bit funny, depending on your sense of humor, it exposed one of the first DE&I pitfalls' companies fall into—inauthenticity in their diversity efforts.

Rent-A-Minority.com proved that several organizations just want a quick fix that proves to the world that they're not racist, sexist, or homophobic but rather progressive and inclusive.

The desire for a quick fix however, is understandable.

Diversity is in serious demand.

In addition to career development, work-life balance, and remote work, diversity has emerged as a critical consideration for many job seekers when pursuing their ideal workplace and later a factor that contributes to employee retention (Yello, 2018).

Emerging talent, referring to Millennials and Gen Z, especially tend to favor diverse workplaces (Kochhar, 2016).

Pay and benefits are only getting companies so far, top talent seek out companies where they believe they're going to be heard, valued, appreciated, given autonomy, and invested in. A lack of representation can be seen as a red flag that indicates a hierarchical and unequal culture.

Consumers are also starting to expect large corporations to step-up and use their power and influence to take a stance on social issues pertaining to historical oppression in addition to prioritizing representation within their workforce.

Accordingly, investors are starting to consider the long-term financial repercussions for organizations that fail to maintain a workforce that is representative of society at large. Evidence of recruiting, retention, and promotions is becoming an application requirement and a factor in decision making for investors (Pinilla & Hampole, 2020). Consequently, investors are displaying less willingness to invest in companies that don't meet their diversity criteria.

Nasdaq Inc. announced back in 2020 that most companies listed on its US stock exchange will be required to include a minimum of two "diverse" directors, one who identifies as female and another who identifies as an "underrepresented minority or LGBTQ" (Nguyen et al., 2020).

Companies are under increasing pressure to take a stance, become fully transparent regarding the composition of diversity within their workforce, and to achieve a surface-level definition of diversity.

In order to comply and meet expectations, companies attempt to quantify their current diversity by taking the data stored in their software system such as employees' age, sex, nationality, seniority in the company, pay grade, and other details (depending on the organization and country) and put it all into info-graphics, dashboards, and annual diversity reports.

If they're not quantifiably diverse enough, they're compelled to increase their representation before facing public criticism.

Executives and leaders turn to ambitious diversity targets, hiring campaigns, marketing, public quotas/commitments, and initiatives as solutions to enhance their organization's image in terms of diversity and inclusion.

A significant portion of the initial steps taken towards achieving diversity goals is done through superficial means of showcasing current employees who belong to historically marginalized groups, as opposed to considering deeper challenges and, therefore, solutions to diversity.

I have observed numerous companies quickly gather their minority employees for events, photos, or marketing videos or invite a minority guest speaker to an event or public speaking engagement, in a last minute effort to showcase diversity.

During my time working overseas, I was frequently asked to partake in panel discussions and interviews for my former employer. Not only did my proficiency in English make me a viable candidate, but my status as a young woman in a male-dominated, older demographic was used as a symbol of change.

These tools, metrics, and use of imagery can be great at providing transparency, attracting diverse candidates, and tracking the progress of organizational efforts which have been intended to uproot systemic bias in the workplace; however, numbers in reports, or temporarily showcasing, targeting, and attracting more underrepresented groups doesn't automatically guarantee success in achieving authentic, long-term diversity.

None of those things ensures productive collaboration, a positive working environment that's conducive to the retention of all talent, nor is any one of them a long-term solution to an organization's diversity challenges.

The real question we should be asking ourselves is this: Does putting people into categories and targeting individuals based on physical differences really do anyone justice?

I've personally witnessed how overcompensating with inauthentic diversity efforts and focusing on quick hiring wins in terms of representation can actually further institutionalize discrimination and lead to unintended negative outcomes.

Following my presentation of the comprehensive diversity study I had conducted at the company I worked for overseas, emphasizing the adoption of inclusive practices to foster greater diversity for the future, the organization ultimately made the decision to channel their efforts towards the development of a targeted diversity campaign.

In other words, rather than considering initiatives aimed at tackling some of the systemic issues within the working culture, based on employee feedback, in order to support the current minorities within the organization and create a more inclusive culture that organically attracted diverse talent, the organization invested in better marketing.

The goal of the campaign was to attract more diverse candidates to the organization through showcasing individuals who represented a variety of different characteristics of diversity.

Several women and the one employee at the company in a wheelchair out of the 6,000 employees at that location were strategically placed in videos and photos to be used in marketing materials, to represent how inclusive an organization it was and the opportunities available for individuals of all sexes, races, ages, and physical abilities.

Now, I understand that the organization had the best intentions for attracting more diversity; however, what they were displaying wasn't an accurate representation of the people the company actually employed.

The false advertising of whom the company was composed set up the individuals who were attracted to apply, based on the campaign, with unrealistic expectations.

The campaign however, did in fact successfully attract a group of more diverse candidates.

Soon after the release, there was a substantial influx of new diverse hires, many of whom lasted less than a year.

Simply using current minorities to attract other minorities didn't solve any of the current challenges women and other underrepresented groups had been facing within that organization.

In fact, it rather exacerbated them and caused much disappointment for the individuals who had been attracted under the false pretense that they were going to have a great experience as a female and/or minority.

Disingenuous attempts at DE&I aren't necessarily flying under the radar anymore either.

Over the years, numerous organizations have found themselves under fire for inauthentic marketing efforts or their lack of genuine support behind DE&I commitments.

Back in 2022, Walmart got themselves into trouble selling Juneteenth ice cream. While the company sells other Juneteenth-themed items, the decision to commercialize the holiday by selling Great Value branded Juneteenth ice cream was met with public scrutiny. Many people viewed it as profiting from a holiday meant to memorialize the end of slavery and took to social media calling out the company's insensitivity.

Remember Pepsi's commercial featuring Kendall Jenner during a Black Lives Matter protest? The ad portrayed Pepsi as a solution to societal issues, which was seen as unrealistic and rather distasteful. Pun intended. Viewers criticized the advertisement for trivializing the real issues at play.

Several companies had been quick to release statements and shared intentions to implement new policies to address racial, ethnic, and gender inequality and increase representation among their employee ranks after the murder of George Floyd back in 2020.

However, after their initial displays of intent, most failed to follow through and make much progress, resulting in significant financial repercussions.

Close to 40 lawsuits have been filed against employers that have failed to achieve the DE&I related promises they made, by various employees, investors, and stakeholders who feel betrayed by the unfulfilled DE&I promises made (Hood, 2023).

Experts are saying there could be even more lawsuits on the horizon if companies continue to fail to fully integrate their DE&I pledges into their workforce and board-level operations.

These incidents highlight the importance of considering historical and social contexts when taking a stance on issues, actively listening to consumer feedback, and avoiding oversimplification of complex social issues.

You don't have to be a lawyer or a rocket scientist to figure out that not only will genuine and authentic diversity efforts pay off as a good thing for business and society overall but they might also help avoid a hefty lawsuit and a Pandora's box of other difficulties.

I'll write it as many times as I have to, but there is no quick fix for diversity, equity, or inclusion.

Authentic diversity, equity, and inclusion in the workplace requires a sustained and dedicated effort.

It's not something that can be achieved by throwing money into one-off campaigns or superficial displays of diversity.

In the face of mounting pressure to display overt diversity, it is imperative to recognize and embrace your organization's current position, placing authenticity and follow-through as top priorities above all else. By acknowledging your starting point, you can then focus on uncovering areas for improvement and implementing genuine measures that organically foster a more diverse environment in the future.

Any meaningful progress in DE&I is going to require the willingness to acknowledge and tackle complex as well as sometimes even messy organizational challenges head-on. In addition, there needs to be unwavering faith and commitment to the long haul.

This means facing difficult conversations, acknowledging and rectifying any biases or discriminatory practices prevalent within the organization, and actively seeking diverse perspectives and voices across all levels of the company to understand real needs.

DE&I is never going to be achieved through a fleeting investment. It demands a long-term investment in sustainable solutions that nurture a workplace culture of support and empowerment for all employees.

Key Takeaways:

- Don't inquire about the services of Rent-A-Minority. com, the website was intended to be a joke and wouldn't work for your organization long-term anyways.

- Temporary representation does not address or solve deep-rooted diversity, equity, and inclusion issues.

- While public commitments to DE&I and marketing efforts may temporarily satisfy talent, consumers, and investors, thoughtless marketing, inaccurate representation, or unfulfilled commitments can quickly backfire and potentially lead to lawsuits or public scrutiny against your organization.

- Resist succumbing to pressure to instantly achieve overt diversity or take stances on issues. Instead, embrace your organization's current position, prioritize authenticity, follow-through, and acknowledge the need for improvement to foster a more diverse environment organically.

- True progress in DE&I requires genuine and sustained investment and effort.

Reflection Questions:

1. Has your organization publicly pledged any commitments to promoting diversity, equity, or inclusion? Why do you think your organization has or hasn't taken these steps?

2. Have you witnessed instances where your organization has faced negative consequences due to inaccurate representation or unfulfilled commitments to DE&I?

3. In what ways can your organization resist the pressure to achieve instant and overt diversity and instead focus on authentic progress?

4. How can your organization align its public commitments to DE&I with meaningful actions and follow-through?

5. How do you perceive your organization's readiness to engage in introspective work and confront biases through open and potentially uncomfortable conversations?

6. What steps can your organization take to foster a culture that values and supports diversity, equity, and inclusion in the long run?

7. How committed is your organization to making sustained investments and efforts towards achieving genuine diversity and inclusion?

CAUGHT IN A REACTIVE CYCLE RATHER THAN TAKING A PROACTIVE APPROACH TO DE&I

If you've ever seen the movie *Hidden Figures*, the American biographical drama film directed by Theodore Melfi and written by Melfi and Allison Schroeder, then you surely remember the pivotal moment that NASA realized the inefficiency of segregation.

For those of you who haven't seen the movie, spoiler alert, at one point, one of the White male bosses at NASA humiliates one of the female African American employees asking her where she is most of the day since she's never at her desk when he needs her.

Out of frustration and in front of everyone, she lists several of the challenges she faces as a segregated woman of color including the fact that there are no "colored bathrooms" in the vicinity for her to use, forcing her to walk forty minutes every time she needs to relieve herself.

After she was finished, everyone in the room was left speechless.

They appeared to be oblivious to the considerable disadvantage women of color experienced due to the tolerated segregation in the office.

The very next scene of the movie shows the boss annihilating the "Whites only" sign above the nearest female bathroom with a crowbar.

When he's done, he tells all the employees very blatantly that everyone pees the same color and that NASA will no longer have segregated bathrooms.

This is such a powerful scene, but shows how, historically, workplace diversity efforts have been implemented in response to some type of problem rather than proactively planned.

The reason for this is rooted in the historical context of workplace diversity initiatives, which were originally established as a response to civil rights movements and as a means of complying with affirmative action requirements (Vaughn, 2018).

From an American perspective, diversity in the workplace can be traced back to the Second World War. At that time, many women entered the workforce to accommodate the major labor force shortages caused by the military draft.

The number of women in the workplace reached new heights during the 1940s, but opportunities and progress for women in their careers were stifled as men rejoined the workforce over the following decades. This later fueled protests and campaigns for more equal opportunities for women.

Also, in the 1940s, President Truman signed Executive Order 9981, which was the first legal move to desegregate the United States Army, which had been segregated mainly based on ethnicity up until that point.

This order is considered to be the first legislation regarding "diversity in the workplace" and paved the way for similar initiatives across industries.

Fast forward to the civil rights movement of the 1960s. This offered more opportunities and created space for cultural and ethnic diversity in the workplace. However, comparable to gender diversity, it took several decades for employers to fully understand the value of diversity initiatives based on cultural background or ethnicity.

Education and diversity training have been a staple of diversity and inclusion work since the 1960s. In its infancy, diversity training mainly focused on race, coinciding with the civil rights movements at that time.

The most common diversity training was facilitated by a Black and White duo of male facilitators, who would introduce the two perspectives and demonstrate interracial collaboration.

The role of the White facilitator was to openly display emotions about their own journey in recognizing systemic racism and their own biases.

It is important to remember how overtly people of color were being discriminated against back in the 1960s, as well as women and anyone else outside the stereotypical White male.

Because the training was used to initiate radical change, confrontation was extremely common, particularly toward White Americans who "gave excuses for" or "denied their racism."

The goal was to increase White American sensitivity to the effects of racial inequity and lay a stepping stone to achieve equality within organizations in a world that has historically oppressed those with less social, political, and economic power. However, this approach generally only resulted in one of three outcomes:

1. Participants gained deeper insights about the barriers to race relations as a result of being put on the hot seat.

2. Participants became more resistant to racial harmony as they fought against accepting the facilitators' label of them as racists.

3. Participants became fanatics and started to advocate against any perceived form of racial injustice after the training.

Starting in the 1970s and increasingly into the 1990s, women began entering the workforce more frequently in industries that were primarily dominated by men. As a result, gender sensitivity training of a similar fashion started to become more prevalent.

While cultural diversity efforts and progress became stagnant, the feminist movement of the 1970s prompted women in the US to take a much larger share of management positions between 1980 and 2010.

Initially, businesses largely relied on diversity initiatives and education to protect themselves against, and even settle, civil rights lawsuits.

Over the years, there has been a significant increase in education, initiatives, and laws aimed at addressing bias and discrimination against various other identity groups, including those based on differences in age, ability, religion, sexual orientation, and even body type.

Today, several corporations have made diversity training a routine practice.

Many employers require their employees to attend truly riveting annual training sessions, during which someone from Human Resources lists the various protected classes via PowerPoint presentations, reminding employees that discrimination is both unethical and illegal.

Although I may be somewhat sarcastic about the repetitive and mundane training that HR puts employees through, it is important for employers to maintain a focus on addressing current issues and confronting historical biases that prevail.

Despite the progress made since the 1940s, women and other minority groups still face oppression and are significantly underrepresented, especially in executive positions, across industries.

This lack of representation at the top perpetuates barriers for individuals who don't fit into a standard mold.

While several organizations continue to use training as a way to acknowledge and address bias, its elusive nature and lack of quantifiability make it a challenge to prioritize from a business perspective. One computer simulation, however, revealed how the cumulative effect of even the smallest expression of bias can impact the representation of men and women within an organization (Sleek, 2018).

The simulation began with equal representation of men and women across eight "hierarchical" levels. Level 1 represented the most junior level at a company and 8 was the most senior.

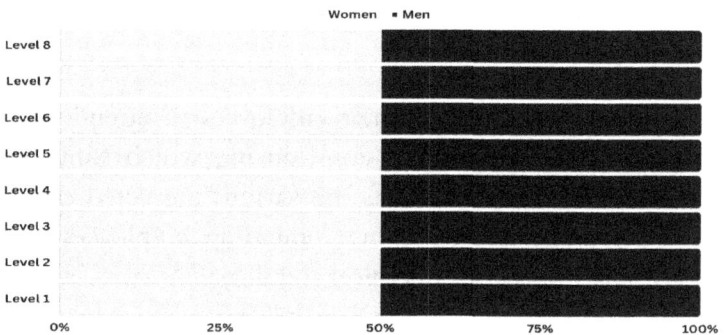

To account for turnover, the researcher calculated 15% attrition at every level. The way that attrition was filled was to promote someone from the level below, based on their performance score.

Everyone in the simulation had a randomly generated performance score; however, the researcher programmed 1% of the variance in those performance scores, biased against women.

In other words, performance scores for women ranged anywhere from 1–100 and performance scores for men ranged anywhere from 1–101.

The simulation was repeated until every original member of the organization was replaced by someone new. The final results were averaged across the twenty iterations.

The study's findings indicated that even a modest 1% of bias in performance evaluations can skew the gender distribution at the top to 35% female and 65% male. (Sleek, 2018)

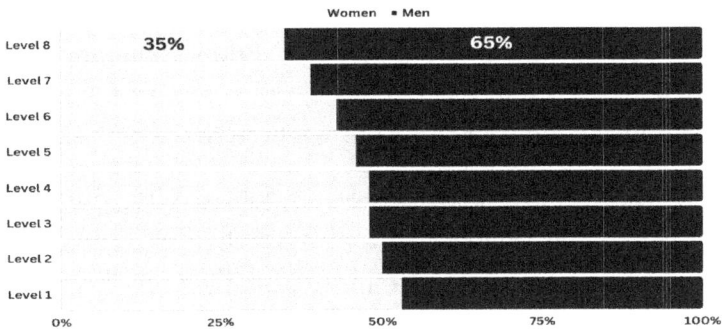

Women ■ Men

Level 8	35%	65%
Level 7		
Level 6		
Level 5		
Level 4		
Level 3		
Level 2		
Level 1		
0%	25%	50%	75%	100%

These numbers are fairly consistent with the number of women in corporate positions worldwide. Reports are published every year that highlight the progress that still needs to be made to achieve global gender equality.

While there are certainly other factors that contribute to underrepresentation of women, especially at executive levels, it would be unrealistic to deny the impact of bias and the lack of representation perpetuating these disparities.

The World Economic Forum (2016) ran a study to identify the most significant obstacles that women face in their careers.

According to the findings, the top reported barrier women identified was bias, which encompassed a range of issues such as the perception that competent women are less likable, the belief that women's success was the result of hard work rather than skill, and assumptions that women are less committed to their careers (World Economic Forum, 2016).

This phenomenon applies to not only women but also other underrepresented groups.

Various studies across the world have revealed that job applicants with names perceived as "Ethnic-sounding" are often at a disadvantage and less likely to receive follow up communication regarding their applications.

For instance, in the United States, job seekers with perceived "Black-sounding" names were often overlooked by prospective employers, irrespective of their qualifications and skills (Leonard, 2018).

Similarly, in Germany, applicants with German names were more likely to receive a response from employers for an interview, especially in the case of smaller firms, compared to applicants with Turkish-sounding names ("Study Finds Major Discrimination," 2010).

A lack of representation of diverse talent can present significant obstacles for minorities to even enter a homogeneous workforce. Furthermore, minorities who are brought into such environments can face limited opportunities for career progression over time.

This has been an anomaly for decades that laws in tandem with DE&I initiatives have been working to combat, which only underscores the ongoing importance of DE&I education and efforts that aim to minimize bias and support previously oppressed minority groups.

However, the mistake lies in the fact that corporate DE&I efforts beyond the annual obligatory training typically only happen as a reaction to something. Whether its problems or conflicts brought to HR's attention, public pressure stemming from prominent movements like Black Lives Matter or #MeToo, or lawsuits.

Companies pretend to be proactive when they change their profile picture on social media to show support for causes such as Black Lives Matter or events like Pride Month, some even make pledges to improve their DE&I efforts in response to said issues. But when the hype dies down, it becomes apparent that these actions were merely gestures and it's back to business as usual.

This reactive approach undermines the importance of ongoing efforts and fails to create any lasting impact.

Case in point, Wells Fargo recently found themselves in the midst of yet another scandal. This time, grappling with no less than five lawsuits from shareholders who claim that the bank's board conveniently acted on DE&I issues only after negative media coverage had exposed them (Hudson, 2023).

Even though the bank's CEO, Charlie Scharf, initiated a 'Diverse Search Requirement' program back in 2020 (around the time George Floyd was murdered), which made interviews with diverse candidates a requirement for positions that paid more than $100,000 per year, the lawsuits indicated that the organization continued to violate basic federal anti-discrimination laws.

In the case of NASA, they were able to recognize the waste of time and money that the lack of diversity, equity, and inclusion was costing them without any media coverage or legal actions.

Both instances however, demonstrate that it took uncomfortable and confrontational moments to compel these organizations to acknowledge the detrimental impact of inadequate diversity, equity, and inclusion, both in terms of wasted time and financial resources. Only then did they take necessary corrective action.

This shouldn't have to be the norm.

Of course, there should be continued efforts that attempt to address the impact of the unfortunate historical oppression and consequential bias regarding individuals in protected classes; And certainly, there will always be a place for diversity and sensitivity training in the workplace to hold individuals accountable.

However, taking a continuous reactive approach to diversity, equity, and inclusion not only undermines an organization's credibility but also creates the impression that they're only committed to taking real action when forced to do so by external pressure.

Everyone has different life circumstances, challenges, and assumptions about them based on their characteristics such as age, sex, or race that they're up against while managing their career.

Some people may have long commutes, limited access to resources or amenities that are considered basic in the twenty-first century, or strenuous family responsibilities outside of work.

It's not always possible to see or understand these circumstances at a glance, especially in an office setting, and you may never truly know what your colleagues might be dealing with underneath the surface.

Nevertheless, all employees should be supported in such a way that they are set up for success within their role.

Examples of providing proactive equal opportunity can include closer parking spaces for pregnant employees, encouraging employees to take advantage of remote working and flexible working hours, providing a list of babysitters in the area, or offering longer-term childcare options for parents who need to go on business trips or want to participate in evening team events.

In order to fully embrace a proactive approach, organizations must transcend surface-level differences and acknowledge the invaluable unique experiences that each employee brings to the table, fostering an environment where every employee feels a sense of responsibility to offer creative solutions and support their colleagues in enhancing their performance whenever possible.

Key Takeaways:

- Corporate DE&I efforts originated from the historical oppression of women and minorities and were largely initially implemented to comply with affirmative action requirements.

- Uncomfortable and confrontational moments should not be the only things that compel organizations to acknowledge the detrimental impact of inadequate diversity, equity, and inclusion, leading to corrective action and a realization of wasted time and financial resources.

- There will always be a place for annual as well as reactive corporate diversity training as women and other minority groups continue to face bias that affects their career advancement.

- Solely prioritizing reactive diversity training and superficial support for social movements when they are trending, without upholding consistent proactive efforts however, will yield no significant progress.

- All employees face challenges, and in order to gain any real traction, companies must take a proactive approach to DE&I initiatives and commit to ongoing efforts to address bias and inequality within the workplace.

Reflection Questions:

1. How does your organization prioritize and schedule DE&I training sessions? Is it done regularly or on an ad hoc basis?

2. What specific topics or areas of focus do your corporate training programs cover regarding DE&I?

3. From your perspective, how effective are your organization's current corporate diversity efforts? Are they effectively addressing the needs of employees?

4. To what extent does your organization demonstrate an understanding of and address the unique challenges faced by different groups within the workforce?

5. How committed is your organization to taking proactive measures in addressing bias and promoting equality? Can you provide examples of such initiatives?

6. How do you perceive the alignment between reactive support for social movements and consistent, long-term proactive efforts in promoting diversity and inclusion within your organization?

LIMITING THE DEFINITION
OF DIVERSITY TO
SUPERFICIAL FEATURES

The company I was working for at the time had just hired its first-ever female board member.

This was a huge milestone for the over 100-year-old organization.

She was given the title, Chief of People Officer, and her role was to support the cultural transformation, starting with the HR department.

After her first few weeks as CPO, she invited the entire HR department to a one-day team builder offsite.

The goals of the day were to do some team building, address current departmental challenges, and announce as well as co-create upcoming initiatives for the rest of the year.

Within minutes of her opening presentation, she announced that diversity was something she wanted the department to work on, moving forward. Recent company data had exposed that the organization was largely composed of White males, with very little internationality throughout.

She described how, in her experience, diverse teams had always outperformed and made collaboration far more fruitful.

It was all sounding fantastic until one of the gentlemen raised his hand and asked in a skeptical manner, "Do we have a definition of diversity?"

This question appeared to have caught her off guard.

Think about it for a moment. What comes to your mind when you think about diversity?

Often, superficial features such as skin color, sex, or any other apparent unique feature that deviates from a standard White male are generally considered diverse.

We've been conditioned in our professional environments to focus on overt physical differences.

Diversity workshops and presentations have long overused imagery of multicolor hands holding one another, holding the world up, or doing some type of collaborative action like high-fiving.

The way our brains typically imagine diversity is often based on a cliché stock-photo version of a diverse group.

We can so easily jump to the conclusion that in order for a team to be truly diverse, they must distinctly represent nearly every single race on the planet.

The gentleman's question intended to clarify if the new Chief of People Officer's expectations for diversity were based simply on superficial characteristics.

While the CPO did have legitimate points in her opening statement, industry thought leaders unanimously conclude that diversity in terms of sex and race is a competitive advantage and drives many of the metrics that shareholders care about.

McKinsey found that teams in which men and women are equal earn up to 41% more revenue, culturally diverse teams outperform by up to 33%, and companies with the most ethnically/culturally diverse boards worldwide are 43% more likely to experience higher profits (Hunt, 2018).

However, she was unintentionally reducing diversity to apparent physical differences and making a large portion of the current workforce feel invaluable and undesirable as a result.

This is yet another common pitfall that many business professionals and companies can easily step into.

On a day-to-day basis, it can be easy to forget just how complex the concept of diversity really is.

If you take another moment to really think about it, there are practically an infinite number of characteristics each human can possess, at any given time, that contribute to their uniqueness.

To get a better grasp on the concept of diversity, academia has identified and broken it down into four distinct components. These components include internal diversity, external diversity, organizational diversity, and worldview diversity. (Alliant International University, 2020)

Internal Diversity

Internal diversity refers to characteristics that are related to situations that a person is born into. Because we're born into them, they're out of our control and, therefore, impossible to choose or change.

Some examples of internal diversity include:

Sex

Sex refers to biological and genetic differences between male and female bodies.

For a quick refresh in biology: females have two X chromosomes and males have one X and one Y chromosome. These biological differences are what we have historically used to categorize individuals as either male or female.

However, the concept of sex can be more complex than a simple binary classification, as some individuals are born with variations in their reproductive and sexual anatomy that don't conform to typical male or female characteristics.

These individuals are described as intersex and can have a range of biological traits that fall between the traditional male/female categories. As a result, sex can be viewed as a spectrum rather than a strict binary division.

Sexual Orientation

Sexual orientation refers to a person's inherent and enduring emotional, romantic, or sexual attraction to other individuals.

This attraction can be directed toward people of the same gender (homosexual), opposite gender (heterosexual), both genders (bisexual), or all genders (pansexual).

Age

Age refers to the amount of time that has elapsed after an individual is born.

The time period in which we're born into has its own set of social, political, and economic conditions that shape our upbringing and significantly influence the values, morals, and expectations of each generation.

Disability Status

A disability is any condition of the body or mind that makes it more difficult or limits the person with the condition to do certain activities.

While the term disability is often used as a catch-all phrase that refers to a single group of people, the reality is that the range of disabilities is quite diverse and refers to individuals with wide ranging abilities and needs.

Disability can include but is not limited to impairment of body structure or function, mental abilities, activity limitations that affect basic functions such as sight, hearing, walking, or problem solving, and participation restrictions that hinder individuals from carrying out daily activities such as work or engaging in social or recreational endeavors.

Neurodiversity

Neurological differences refer to variations in the structure or function of a person's nervous system that affect the way they process and respond to sensory information, thoughts, and emotions.

These differences can be a result of genetics, disease, or environmental influences.

Some examples of neurological differences include Autism spectrum disorder (ASD), Attention deficit hyperactivity disorder (ADHD), Dyslexia, Tourette syndrome, or Epilepsy.

Race

Race, although commonly confused with ethnicity, is primarily based on a person's inherent biological characteristics such as bone structure, skin color, hair type, and eye color.

These physical features have historically been used to label and further categorize humans.

Common racial categories in the United States include Black or African American, White, Native American, or Alaskan Native, Asian, and Pacific Islander.

Cultural Background

Cultural background encompasses the customs, traditions, and beliefs that shape an individual's worldview and behavior. This includes factors such as food, language, religion, and other cultural practices that are shared among a group of people.

External Diversity

The second category of diversity is known as external diversity, which includes characteristics that are influenced by a person's environment or circumstances and may change over time.

These characteristics are often shaped or imposed by external factors, such as societal norms, cultural practices, and personal experiences.

Some examples of external diversity include:

Ethnicity

Unlike race, ethnicity is determined by learned behaviors and cultural factors such as geographic background, nationality, regional culture, ancestry, and language.

While race is largely determined by biology and physical characteristics, ethnicity is shaped by the social and cultural groups to which people belong.

Examples of ethnic groups include Hispanic or Latino, Middle Eastern/Arab or European (such as German, Irish, Italian, etc.).

Gender Identity

Gender identity is an individual's innermost sense of their own gender.

This may or may not correspond to the sex with which they were assigned at birth that was based on their physical anatomy.

Gender identity can be fluid and is subject to change over time. It is determined by an individual based on how they perceive themselves and how they wish to be perceived by others.

Beyond the male and female binaries, there is a wide spectrum of gender identities that individuals may identify with including non-binary, transgender, genderqueer, genderfluid, and demigender, ungendered, agender, genderless, or gender-free.

Gender Expression

Gender expression is an aspect of gender that might differ from an individual's sex that was assigned to them at birth or even their gender identity.

It specifically refers to how an individual expresses their gender identity through their external appearance.

Gender expression can be communicated in a variety of different ways, including through clothing, hairstyles, makeup, behavior, mannerisms, and preferred pronouns.

Social Roles

Social roles are expectations and behaviors that are imposed on individuals based on their demographics, such as age, gender, and cultural background. They are social constructs that can have a significant impact on individuals' experiences and opportunities.

Gender roles are a prominent example of social roles that are often based on an individual's sex that was assigned at birth. Adult women might be expected to assume primary childcare and domestic responsibilities, while men may be expected to prioritize their careers and provide for their families.

Social roles and expectations can vary considerably across cultures and societies and can even change over time.

Family and Upbringing

Family structure and upbringing can have a significant impact on a person's life.

Whether the structure is nuclear, extended, single-parent, or blended family, plays a crucial role in shaping an individual's upbringing, and can determine the type of support and responsibilities they have throughout their life. Regardless of their family situation, everyone has obligations and bonds with those they care about.

Early experiences in childhood can shape an individual's beliefs about themselves, others, and the world, and can lead to the formation of both functional and dysfunctional behaviors.

These experiences can have a lasting impact that carry into adulthood.

Education

Education is the process of acquiring knowledge, skills, values, and attitudes through various methods such as teaching, training, research, or practical experience. It is a lifelong process that begins at a young age and continues throughout one's lifetime.

Formal education is typically acquired through schools or universities, and varies greatly based on location, school, and teacher. The quality of a person's education is largely influenced by national, state, and district laws or requirements.

Informal education is acquired through personal experiences, reading, or self-directed learning. Informal education is most often self-initiated and self-directed and can occur in various settings such as the workplace, community centers, or online courses.

Work Experience

Work experience refers to the skills, knowledge, and practical experience that an individual accumulates through their previous employment or work-related activities.

The flavor of that experience is largely influenced by the identity and values of the organizations they've worked for.

For example, one company might prioritize innovation, trying new things, and creativity, while another might prioritize tradition, accuracy, and precision. These differences are largely influenced by factors such as the company's size, geographic location, and the industry it operates in.

Skills

Skills refer to the ability of an individual to perform a specific task or job.

Skills and competencies can be technical or non-technical. They are acquired and developed over time through various methods such as training, practice, and experience.

Examples of technical skills include data analysis, programing, or engineering. Nontechnical skills are referred to as soft skills and can include communication, problem solving, and critical thinking.

Personality

Personality is the culmination of characteristics or qualities that form an individual's distinct character. Personalities elicit information about a person's motivations, preferences, interests, emotional make-up, and style of interacting with people and situations.

There are several parameters that can be used to describe and define a person's personality.

Personality tests, such as the Myers-Briggs Type Indicator (MBTI), Enneagram (which identifies nine different personality types), and Typefinder (which identifies sixteen different personality types), can be used to further measure and describe different aspects of a person's personality.

Organizational diversity

The third category of diversity is Organizational Diversity.

Organizational diversity refers to the differences between individuals assigned to them by their organization.

Some examples of organizational diversity include:

Employment Status

Employment status refers to the current status of an individual's employment.

This can include factors such as whether they are employed or unemployed, their job title or position, whether they work full time or part time, and whether they are a contracted worker or employed as a regular employee.

Employment status can have implications on various aspects of an individual's life, including the amount of income they earn, benefits, job security, and overall career prospects.

Management Status

Management status refers to an individual's position or level within an organization's management hierarchy.

Depending on the organization, management status can range from first-level managers who directly supervise employees, to middle level managers who oversee entire departments or business units, all the way to top-level executives such as CEOs who make strategic decisions for the entire organization.

Management status is often determined by factors such as job responsibilities, level of authority, decision-making power, and degree of accountability.

Pay grade

Pay grade is a hierarchical level assigned to a job or position within an organization, generally based on job responsibilities, required skills, and experience.

Each pay grade corresponds to a predetermined range of salary or wage that is associated with the job or position.

Worldview diversity

The final category of diversity is Worldview Diversity, which encompasses an individual's perspective that evolves over time through their life experiences.

Some examples of worldview diversity include:

Life Experiences

Life experiences encompass all of the unique private and public occurrences an individual undergoes throughout their lifetime.

Examples include military experiences, childbirth, or immersing oneself in another culture.

The accumulation of one's life experiences contributes to who they are, how they view the world, and how they interact with others.

Religious and Spiritual Beliefs

Religious beliefs are practices and rituals that pertain to belief in a higher being. Religious practices can include prayer, wearing a cross as a symbol of faith, covering one's head or whole body, or engaging with a religious community.

Spiritual beliefs or spirituality is the recognition of a higher being, greater than one's self. Spirituality may or may not involve involvement in a spiritual community and is related to an existential perspective on life, death, and the nature of reality.

Ideologies

Ideologies are a set of beliefs, values, and principles that shape an individual's worldview and guide their actions and decision making.

They provide a framework for interpreting and understanding the world around us, and often include political, social, and economic perspectives.

Ideologies can be both positive and negative, depending on one's point of view, and can be associated with different movements, organizations, or political parties.

Examples of ideologies include Liberalism, Conservatism, Socialism, Capitalism, Feminism, Environmentalism, and Nationalism.

Conflict and division can arise when the ideologies of two individuals clash and cause them to compete for power and influence.

Morals

Morals are personal beliefs as to what is deemed acceptable and unacceptable.

Morals are also often informed by cultural, religious, or philosophical beliefs, and can vary between individuals and societies.

Morals can encompass a wide range of behaviors, including honesty, fairness, compassion, respect, and responsibility. They're often taught and reinforced through socialization, education, and religious or cultural practices.

Morals can influence how individuals interact with others, how they navigate moral dilemmas, and how they form ethical judgments. They can also play a role in shaping societal and organizational norms and policies.

As you have probably gathered by now, the categories of diversity explained in this chapter are quite extensive. However, the examples provided only scratch the surface as to just how different we all are and only provide a glimpse into the complexity of our unique identities and experiences.

In fact, attempting to fully articulate the extent of our differences would be a nearly impossible task.

Even individuals who grew up in the same town, went to the same school, are of the same sex, and are of the same race can have significant differences between them.

This just shows that diversity is just as complex and diverse as what it alludes to and we are all far more complex and exceptional beyond characteristics such as our sex, race, or nationality.

Sincere diversity is the attempt to understand, appreciate, and leverage whenever possible the limitless combinations of characteristics that make each individual unique.

Now that last sentence sounds phenomenal, I should know because I wrote it. However, it's important that I address that it's not going to be humanly possible to get to know, understand, and therefore consider every aspect of every person's diversity on your team and certainly not within your entire organization.

For obvious reasons, it's not necessarily common to talk about deeper aspects of one's background in the workplace such as upbringing or family structures. Some aspects of ourselves are typically frowned upon altogether as topics of discussion in the workplace such as religious or political beliefs. And it's not every day we consider our own morals; they rather show themselves in our decision making and behaviors. Furthermore, some people may not want to disclose so much about themselves or their background and may have different expectations for how open they want to be in the workplace.

While it may be impossible to fully understand others' entirety, it's still crucial to make an effort to better understand and get to know the people you work with. By doing so, you not only build stronger relationships but also are better prepared to recognize and leverage the unique strengths and characteristics of those around you when opportunities arise.

I had recently seen a successful cross-functional and cross-cultural project being celebrated within the organization I was working in at the time.

Two of the marketing teams, based in different countries, had worked together to create a marketing campaign for a new product in an expanding market.

Their campaign had exceeded all sales expectations and the messaging had appeared to have resonated strongly with consumers in the new market.

The team working on the project had all the traditional characteristics of diversity that are considered to make teams successful. Not only were the team members almost an equal mix of men and women but also all of them varied greatly in terms of age and nationality.

With my limited definition of diversity at the time, I saw this as the perfect opportunity to enhance the business case I was building for the company to invest in greater diversity efforts. So, I immediately asked the team if I could interview them to better understand and convey to the rest of the organization how they were able to collaborate so well together despite their vast differences and locations, and why they thought the project had been such a success.

When they agreed to meet with me, I excitedly put together a group of questions that were looking to extract how working with such a diverse group, despite any challenges that came along with that, ultimately resulted in the project being the huge success that it was.

I frantically wrote down statements as to how fun it was for all of them to collaborate, how they overcame challenges such as the time difference (having been located in different countries with different time zones), and how despite the extra time they spent taking into consideration everyone on the team's perspective, how much more fruitful the project ended up being because of that.

I believed I had all the information I needed when one of the team members stated that the project's outcome likely wouldn't have been as successful without the cultural perspective of the colleagues.

Nevertheless, I still had one more round of interviews to complete.

During my final interview with the last few team members, my perspective was completely shifted.

When speaking to the project manager of the team regarding the impact of diversity on the results of the project, he was not nearly as convinced as I was that the biggest factor that contributed to the success of the project had been representation.

He explained that his primary focus when putting together this team, like any other, was on the knowledge and competencies of the individuals within that team, rather than their gender, nationality, or even location.

The project manager acknowledged that gender and cultural background does oftentimes add additional value and enrich a project's outcome by providing different competencies and perspectives. However, he emphasized that they are not the primary focus of his decision-making process when putting together a team or developing a strategy for a project.

Instead, his approach was centered on familiarizing himself with his colleagues and then objectively selecting the necessary skills and competencies to create the best possible team.

This project had been no different, he sought out the competencies needed from both locations to ensure the team's success.

Rather than promoting the diversity he had orchestrated within his team, the project manager emphasized the importance of objectivity in decision-making and familiarity with coworkers.

Although diversity can make a significant difference to a project's success, in the example I shared, as cultural context obviously enriched the project's outcome; it should never be the sole deciding factor in staffing or hiring decisions.

There are several factors to consider when putting any team together that go beyond visible or surface-level characteristics.

By taking a more holistic and authentic approach to the concept of diversity, we can establish a strong foundation for understanding and openness towards those who are different from us. This, in turn, can promote more objective decision making.

Viewing individuals as talent with their own distinct set of skills and uniqueness will ensure the best fit for projects and positions, in addition to giving opportunities to individuals who may have been previously overlooked based solely on assumptions.

Embracing diversity can be advantageous for individuals, teams, and companies alike as it creates space for different perspectives, leading to increased engagement and better outcomes such as boosted employee engagement and retention, improved decision making, as well as the intangible personal benefits such as personal development.

This will bring us to the next DE&I pitfall, as a greater appreciation of unique differences is not possible without fostering deeper working relationships.

This means employees must take the time to cultivate relationships based on trust, understanding, and vulnerability.

It also means fostering an inclusive environment where everyone is recognized, appreciated, empowered, and respected.

Only then can a company truly leverage the benefits of diversity and achieve greater success as a team.

Key Takeaways:

- Considering factors such as sex, race, or age when thinking about diversity isn't inherently bad or wrong, however limiting our definition of diversity to overt physical differences can have negative implications.

- Stock photo definitions of diversity generally only put individuals into boxes and may cause those who don't fit an overtly diverse profile to feel unwanted or even resentful of those who do meet such criteria.

- Diversity goes so much deeper than characteristics such as sex, race, and nationality that are typically prioritized in organizational DE&I efforts.

- Even though a healthy mix of characteristics such as sex or nationality can add significant value to projects, putting visible diversity at the forefront rather than viewing individuals for their unique talents and considering their full range of expertise only does your organization a disservice.

- Although it isn't feasible to consider every single aspect of your colleagues' diversity in everyday work life, cultivating a deeper appreciation for unique skills and competencies as well as diverse backgrounds can create opportunities for achieving greater success as a team.

- Authentic diversity is the attempt to understand and appreciate the characteristics that make each individual unique and how those differences can be leveraged within a project or role.

- Fostering deeper working relationships based on trust, understanding, and vulnerability is essential for cultivating a culture of inclusivity and achieving greater success as a diverse team.

Reflection Questions:

1. How do you personally define diversity, and how does your organization define it? Are there any differences or similarities between the two perspectives?

2. To what extent do the members of your organization know each other, allowing them to appreciate and leverage each other's skills and unique abilities during projects?

3. Do you believe that every individual within your organization is genuinely acknowledged, valued, empowered, and treated with respect? Are there any groups or individuals who may feel marginalized or underrepresented?

4. How would you assess the current levels of trust, understanding, and vulnerability within your organization's working culture? Are there any areas that need improvement?

5. How can you cultivate a culture that fosters deeper working relationships based on trust, understanding, and vulnerability to promote inclusivity and enhance the success of your team?

NOT INCLUDING THE DIVERSITY THAT'S ALREADY EMPLOYED

I've always given my all in every job I ever had. That dedication helped me maintain a high level of performance, which is something I've always been really proud of.

Although I was a bit intimidated at the thought of working abroad, I was eager to show the company what I was capable of.

In my first role in the marketing department of the organization I worked for overseas, I was assigned the primary responsibility of collecting and revising articles for an internal newsletter.

This was going to be a piece of cake, or so I thought.

Shortly after I had submitted the first batch of broken English articles I had wordsmithed, my supervisor (Who at that time was the head of global marketing. Emphasis on the global part.) directly asked me if I was stupid since it became apparent to her that I was not able to spell in my own language.

Apparently, she didn't realize there was a difference between American and British English.

Her crude leadership style and lack of cultural knowledge was a shock to me as it didn't reflect the cross-cultural, collaborative, and innovative impression the organization had given off when I applied.

Over time, I noticed a recurring pattern of such behavior and intolerance. I started experiencing a rapid increase in discomfort, insecurity, and a growing sense of dread when it came to going to work each day.

I came to realize just how significant the language barrier was in the organization despite having been told it was an English-speaking company, as I was not trusted with any other significant independent work.

My team really only used me when my English language skills came in handy, but, beyond that, I felt as if I was viewed as incompetent and an inconvenience to the group.

Let's just say I didn't stay in that role any longer than I had to and went home crying more often than I care to admit.

When that contract was up, HR decided to pair me with another American supervisor.

I felt so relieved. Finally, I would be around someone who might understand what it's like to be a foreigner in that environment, and I was looking forward to having a much more positive working experience.

This supervisor was in fact much easier to work with; however, over time, I realized that she was up against a lot of the same exclusion problems that I had been facing.

More people would speak English to her, since she was older and had a higher title, but even still she was often excluded in important meetings or projects. She worked from home a lot or called in sick, likely to avoid the discomfort, which unfortunately only fueled office gossip about her.

She would invite me to her house for 'coworking' sessions, where we would eat pizza and just talk like two Americans. Which was awesome… at first, however the novelty quickly faded.

I came to my own conclusion that she had likely given up on her career within the organization and that there was no hope for development or any long-term career for me on her team.

When I shared my concerns regarding my future at the company with her, she advised me to either move to a bigger city that was five hours away where more people spoke English or to go back to the US.

Rather than doing either of those things, I decided to meet with the company lawyer.

I told him everything. How it had taken me nine months and four interviews, as well as my own personal financial investment to relocate. How I had no support from the company and had taken on all the risk to work at an organization that claimed to want international women like me so badly, yet never seemed to have any intentions of really getting to know me, including me, or utilizing any of my skills for that matter.

Out of the kindness of his heart, he called up a new leader who decided to take pity on my situation.

When I finally got to meet with him, we hit it off directly. He didn't seem to mind speaking English and the project he was working on sounded exciting and exactly like what I had hoped for in my career.

I felt like I was finally going to be on a good team with a leader willing to develop me!

My excitement didn't last long.

I came to find out that my new colleagues were quite competitive and didn't have the same open mind as my new supervisor when it came to working with foreigners.

Despite the company policy requiring the use of English language in the office, soon after I joined the team my colleagues decided they were no longer comfortable speaking in English. As a result, I was forced to move locations and sent to a language class to miraculously become fluent in their language while maintaining the tasks required of me in my current role.

They had made sure that my lack of language became the focal point rather than my ability to do the work required on the team. While I was busy in my language course, they were busy supporting my supervisor in meetings and in our projects.

Even though this sabotaging behavior was clear to my supervisor, he chose to prioritize maintaining a sense of peace for the majority and the team's productivity by opting for the path of least resistance. It was two against one, so I was eventually phased out of any teamwork due to the lack of productive collaboration.

Amidst the drama, I was presented with several unique opportunities during my employment. I had the privilege to speak on panels, travel, and had more frequent exposure to executives than some of my colleagues who had been with the company for years. I even had the rare opportunity to go out to a lobster dinner with the entire executive team.

This created the illusion of a successful career, which was likely to appease the CEO's desire to promote diversity.

However, as I was given more opportunities, my colleagues grew even more resentful and jealous of me, and the harassment only got worse. Some felt compelled enough to let me know that I was only given special treatment because I was the company's "token employee."

In my last year of employment, I was essentially given no tasks, spending my days either working on my diversity study or finding other projects for myself to remain relevant.

I was at one of the lowest points in my life.

No matter how I dressed, talked, or behaved I felt like I was never going to be fully accepted into the company's culture. At several points in those almost three years that I worked for this company I doubted my own intelligence and capabilities, which undoubtedly impacted my motivation and performance.

As an individual who takes my career very seriously and has high aspirations, this was devastating and more frustrating than I could ever explain.

Unsurprisingly, I found that I was not alone in my struggles as a young international woman working within the current culture.

I became acquainted with two other young international women who were also facing their own set of challenges.

I found one of them always at her desk during the lunch break when her colleagues would leave to eat together. She confided in me that she had been advised by her supervisor to find another job at an American-based company that would align with her personality more.

The other girl sought me out as she too wanted to develop her language skills with me as she had been working tirelessly on her team to complete every task required of her in addition to becoming fluent in the language. She eventually opened up about the discrimination she was facing in her department and asked for my help in navigating the situation.

Within a year of our meeting, both individuals were forced to part ways with the organization.

Ironically, despite the company's professed emphasis on diversity, they were struggling with retaining the young and diverse talent they had successfully brought into the company.

When I addressed these issues with a colleague in HR, their response merely attributed the higher turnover of young international women to their alleged lack of compatibility with the organization.

This represents yet another notable pitfall organizations encounter in the realm of DE&I, namely the failure to fully acknowledge, value, and leverage the existing diversity within the company.

I look at this pitfall this way, unless your organization is knowingly terrible at hiring, the talent brought in must have possessed at least some of the necessary skills and expertise to contribute to the company's success to be hired in the first place. No organization, regardless of how big they are, should feel comfortable discarding the value of the annual full-time salaries as well as the skills, capacity, and ideas of their employees.

Now, even though I have just made the case for taking a more comprehensive approach to diversity, if there is a clear pattern or even the slightest inclination of exclusion and higher turnover rates among a specific demographic then it is definitely worthwhile to take inventory of the behavior within the company that is likely causing this rather than undervaluing and letting go of current talent (especially minorities that may have had to jump through several hoops to even make it to the organization in the first place) and praying that the next group of diverse hires will work out.

However, going back to taking a broader perspective, as mentioned earlier, when considering diversity from a wider lens, it becomes apparent that most companies are actually inherently quite diverse. However, the challenge lies in effectively leveraging the existing diversity within their current workforce.

Rather than addressing core behavioral aspects that foster inclusion, as mentioned earlier, organizations frequently fixate on visible diversity as the sole solution for addressing inclusivity. This involves focusing on recruitment efforts and offering, most commonly, temporary opportunities to underrepresented minorities in a way that provides them with exposure.

This approach seems logical. In theory, it assumes that by increasing representation within a homogenous workforce and offering greater opportunities to minorities, empathy will naturally increase, a more supportive environment will emerge, and barriers inhibiting the success of minorities will crumble.

While the push for representation might seem like a step toward greater equality and inclusivity, it's crucial to recognize that the presence of more diverse employees within a workforce does not automatically create an inclusive environment that's able to tap into all talent.

In fact, it can have quite the opposite effect, exacerbating tension between colleagues.

Often, solely focusing on recruiting new talent or giving employees unique opportunities based primarily on specific characteristics or minority status, creates a negative impression and hinders the utilization of individuals' full range of skills and competencies.

Diversity backlash is a complex social phenomenon that can occur when diversity efforts are perceived as insincere, tokenistic, or unfair by members of the majority group within a company.

Current, majority members can start to form feelings of resentment, frustration, and even hostility towards the minority group(s) that were favored as a result of the latest diversity efforts/initiatives.

Consequences of diversity backlash include:

- An atmosphere of distrust in the skills and abilities of the minorities recently hired based on initiatives or a recently enforced quota.

- New hires within the targeted minority groups feeling increased pressure to work extra hard to prove themselves.

- Minorities who have already successfully learned how to navigate the organization's culture, needing to relearn how to navigate the new hostility within the environment.

- Other minority employees who were not highlighted in the diversity quota parameters, feeling that the company's efforts signify that they are not as important, and, therefore, feeling excluded or disgruntled.

Pushing hard for diversity without prioritizing inclusion can unintentionally create even more exclusive and disempowering environments that are not fully prepared to take advantage of or retain the unique strengths and perspectives that diversity can offer.

The backlash I experienced serves as a reminder of the potential drawbacks of emphasizing diversity without corresponding efforts toward inclusion and retention.

Diversity targets and initiatives can, in fact, do a great job of breaking down initial barriers and getting more underrepresented individuals in the door; however, even though newly hired minorities might be given a seat at the table, that doesn't exactly ensure their voices will be heard when they speak up.

In other words, simply hiring more women or people of color doesn't guarantee productive collaboration will take place with all members of the organization, nor does it magically increase the number of innovative ideas or company profits.

Now, I understand that my situation was an extreme case. However, companies all over the world make the same mistake of pushing for greater diversity without fostering the inclusive behavior necessary to tap into and retain it.

Exclusion of talent is a phenomenon that's also not always so extreme or obvious. It happens every day and can be so subtle that it often goes unnoticed.

Have you ever been in a meeting where someone had something valuable to contribute but struggled to communicate effectively in the language being used or where someone presented their ideas in a way that didn't resonate with the dominant voices in the room, so they were ignored or dismissed?

These instances are a lot more common than overt acts of exclusion and discrimination, but they accumulate over time and have a significant impact on those who experience them.

Most people have kind intentions toward one another and normally want to achieve the best outcomes for their teams and organizations, but we are all only human and, unfortunately, our behavior gets in our own way of effectively collaborating.

Daily, employees in companies are responsible for a wide range of tasks from making sales and forging partnerships to marketing products and dealing with customers.

Most employees are held accountable for key performance indicators (KPIs) and are required to make quick decisions, prioritize execution, and achieve their goals.

On top of all our responsibilities, the human brain is exposed to millions of bits of information every second.

Just take a minute to consider the sheer amount of information you have to take in, process and act on in a single day. This includes notifications, instant messages, emails, phone calls, etc.

Although we're constantly exposed to exorbitant amounts of information, it's actually only humanly possible to consciously process a fraction of what we're exposed to.

In order to cope, the human brain unconsciously makes shortcuts to make quicker decisions.

While we all want to believe we are rational human beings who make fair judgments, especially in the workplace, the reality is that we're all inherently biased to varying degrees, which can impact our behavior, even if unintentionally.

We seek out things that we know work for the sake of productivity. We favor information that confirms our existing beliefs and dismiss information that challenges what we've known to be true or have experienced in our own lives.

This type of quick processing allows us to react more quickly and make faster, and what we might think at the time, better decisions. After all, we've been taught that swift decision making is far better than analysis paralysis, and while that might be true, this tendency can lead to a closed-minded approach that limits innovation and prevents the consideration of new perspectives.

Bias can run so much deeper than the information we consider and what we dismiss or contemplate when making business decisions.

We're all capable of holding opinions regarding groups of people based on virtually any distinguishable characteristic such as nationality, sex, and even body weight.

Most people are unaware of their own bias, which is referred to as unconscious or implicit bias. However, these beliefs we hold about other groups of people have the potential to influence not only hiring decisions, but also they way we treat people and whose opinions we value.

In all fairness, I think we can admit with some humility that regardless of how much we have traveled or how much time we've spent learning about other cultures, it's a whole other ballgame to work with and interact with people on a consistent basis who come from entirely different backgrounds and have entirely different ways of communication or expectations of how things should be done.

Working with individuals who share similar backgrounds, sense of humor, education levels, experiences, and expectations can feel easier due to the sense of relatability and agreeableness it creates.

Cultural barriers or vast differences between individuals can be uncomfortable, feel extremely foreign or scary to navigate, and create perceived challenges to collaboration.

However, this similarity bias and avoidance of discomfort gets in the way of productive collaboration and constructive conflict that actually fuels innovation and opens us up to opportunities for growth.

Having bias is an extremely human thing and doesn't make us bad people; if it's any consolation, it's actually what helped our ancestors survive.

In the past, such fast thinking and bias were critical for survival. If we didn't pick up on social cues, conform to the group or make fast judgments with regard to the amount of danger we were in, we were quite literally eliminated from the gene pool.

In particular, the association between large animals and danger helped them navigate their environment and saved their lives. Without this form of bias, they would have been some animal's lunch.

Their brains needed to process quickly in order to survive, and today, our brains need to process quickly to navigate our information-heavy environments.

Although such thinking may have brought us to where we are today, it's not conducive to effective collaboration that will result in the innovation necessary to remain competitive.

Recognizing and addressing personal biases is crucial to avoid generalizing and stereotyping entire groups of people so that you can get out of your own way and foster more genuine relationships that contribute to a more inclusive working environment.

Tiffany Jana and Matthew Freeman explain in their book *Overcoming Bias: Building Authentic Relationships Across Differences*, how we form "in-groups" already as children based on the characteristics of the individuals who raised us. Those attributes from our early relationships have a strong influence on our future preferences.

People we allow to be part of our "in-group" are those most comfortable to be around. They get our jokes, understand our history, and are generally similar to us. On the flip side, we often demand more from people who are subconsciously part of our "out-group" in order to trust them. This limits our ability to make genuine connections to those who are dissimilar to us and who don't meet our subconscious expectations.

When we fail to form authentic working relationships, it hinders productive collaboration and compromises the success of the team.

Our actions can and will reflect our personal biases, whether we're aware of them or not, which hampers inclusion.

While some actions can be in the form of overt verbal insults or put-downs, most are attempts at jokes or are unintentional everyday slights.

These actions are generally based on race, sex, or any other characteristic regarding an individual and include but are not limited to sexual objectification, sexist language, discriminatory humor, or projecting assumptions.

Exclusive behavior can generally be categorized into three main types:

What we say.

Our words have the potential to upset, stigmatize, and isolate the people we interact with.

Even comments intended to be compliments such as "Your English is really good!" to an Asian American or comments intended to be a joke such as "You're the whitest black person I know." To a person of color can be extremely offensive and uncomfortable to the individual being told them.

Any verbalized assumption about someone based on their race, religion, or socioeconomic status is a form of bias and only excludes those being referred to.

Even the comment "I don't see color" is considered offensive, although intended, in some cases, as a nondiscriminatory view of the human race, it actually devalues another individual's experience as a person of color.

How we act.

How we behave toward others has the potential to be hurtful or exclusionary.

Writing off what someone has to say when they voice their opinion, making assumptions about others, and not recognizing individuals' accomplishments are all ways we can act exclusively.

What we allow in our environment.

I thank God that we've come a long way since the 1980s when it was commonplace for men to display calendars featuring half-naked women at their desks. However, subtle forms of discrimination can persist in the physical environments we create.

Having a ton of sports memorabilia all over an office environment can feel exclusive to those uninterested. Or only using the names of men throughout history to label meeting rooms can create a sense of exclusion for those who do not identify with or feel represented by those individuals.

While some of these comments or actions can seem subtle and may not seem like a big deal as isolated incidents, or were intended to be compliments, they are nevertheless behaviors that hurt others, bruise trust, and contribute to exclusive environments.

Research has shown that regular exposure to subtle discrimination can, over time, evoke similar symptoms to severe trauma (Nadal, 2018).

Not only does exposure to consistent acts of discrimination negatively impact mental health in others, but one study found a positive correlation between hypervigilance (a higher sense of alertness to one's surroundings) caused by race-based stress and a higher incidence of heart disease among people of color (Hicken, 2014).

These personal health implications undoubtedly lead to performance issues in the workplace and can cause employees to burn out and eventually leave the organization.

Sincere inclusion is the ability to recognize, appreciate, and leverage the differences between individuals; but for inclusion to happen, everyone involved needs to become aware of their behaviors and commit to creating an environment that's built on trust, allowing space for vulnerability, psychological safety, and collaboration.

Diversity can be a beautiful thing, but it takes a whole lot of humility, empathy, communication, and personal development to make it work.

Diversity without inclusion can have significant ramifications that negatively impact an organization's bottom line.

Promoting diversity without having an inclusive working environment will cause talented employees who were attracted to it under the assumption that diversity is valued within the culture, to feel disillusioned and disappointed with the organization.

This disappointment can have significant financial ramifications for the business, including disengagement, loss of performance, and turnover.

Even top talent can lose motivation if they feel their company doesn't actually take into consideration everyone's perspectives, are not challenged enough in their work, or if the purpose of their role within the context of the entire organization is unclear. Lack of inclusion can cause employees to feel disconnected and become disengaged.

Disengaged employees soon become unhappy with their work and/or employer. They no longer exude any extra effort, enthusiasm, or support for the team. They become complacent and noticeably withdraw from the organization.

The detrimental effects of employee disengagement on an organization's financial performance are typically reflected in higher absence rates.

According to "Absenteeism: The Bottom-Line Killer," unscheduled absenteeism is estimated to costs around $3,600 per year for every hourly worker and roughly $2,650 each year per salaried employee (White paper, 2005).

Consistent disengagement and absenteeism quickly lead to a drop in performance. While some disengaged employees can sustain performance through project ownership or inspiration from their personal work ethic, they're generally the exception and not the rule in exclusive environments.

A decline in employee performance directly and significantly affects the overall performance of the business.

Involved employees have clear roles and tasks, easily and effectively collaborate with others when necessary, meet deadlines, produce quality work, build and promote the brand, make sales and ensure positive customer interactions.

Employees who are not engaged underperform, generate less output, and are not contributing their best efforts to the achievement of the company's goals.

This loss of performance can easily become apparent to customers, which can cause them to seek products or services elsewhere if they feel a company is not eager enough to meet their needs or experience bad customer service.

Employees who have been disengaged over a long period of time are either let go, or eventually seek out other employment opportunities on their own in which they feel they will be able to add value.

High turnover rates serve as an indication that there is a lack of inclusion or utilization of talent within an organization.

Turnover has a significant cost for organizations, considering recruitment and on-boarding expenses in addition to the loss of skills, competencies, and experience of previous talent. It's estimated to cost an average of 6 to 9 months of an employee's salary to replace them

("The Cost of Replacing an Employee," 2016).

High turnover will eventually lead to negative employee ratings in public forums. These are red flags that can create a negative perception among potential candidates, dissuading top talents from applying to the organization.

The combined effect of bias and exclusive behavior creates a detrimental cycle that only stifles business potential.

Industry thought leaders unanimously conclude that diversity is a competitive advantage and drives many of the metrics that shareholders care about.

However, Accenture took their research a step further and linked an organization's culture of equality to an increase in employees' willingness and ability to share innovative ideas resulting in higher profitability.

Inclusion and the utilization of diversity was further linked to metrics such as increased brand quality, talent retention, business expansion, improved perceptions of culture, and organic attraction of more diverse talent (Sweet & Shook, 2020).

Diversity as a competitive advantage can only be achieved if all individuals within the organization are perceived as equals, have strong working relationships, and effort is made to negate bias.

Rather than focusing solely on representation or the promotion of diverse talent, the key to successful collaboration lies in simply getting out of our own way and including and maximizing the potential of the already inherently diverse and qualified talent currently present within your company on a consistent basis.

Key Takeaways:

- Organizations that prioritize diversity without giving equal efforts toward inclusion are missing out on the benefits of having a diverse workforce.

- While diversity is important, inclusion is the key to unlocking the full potential of diversity in the workplace.

- An inclusive environment empowers employees to bring their full selves to work and invites everyone to fully engage, ultimately resulting in greater productivity, and overall success for the organization.

- Bias and human behavior is ultimately what inhibits inclusion, which is why it's important for organizations to actively address and combat these issues.

- Sincere inclusion is the ability to recognize, appreciate, and leverage the differences between individuals; but for inclusion to happen, everyone involved needs to become aware of their behaviors and commit to creating an environment that's built on trust, allowing space for vulnerability, psychological safety, and collaboration.

- Pushing for diversity without inclusion can have serious consequences, leading to poor performance, burnout, and even health issues among employees. This can result in higher absenteeism, lower productivity, and increased turnover rates, ultimately impacting the bottom line of the organization.

- To create an inclusive work environment, there must be a mutual understanding that all ideas and insights are respected, taken into consideration, and implemented when feasible. This facilitates equal access to opportunities, resources, and an overall shift of power within an organization that's able to realize the full potential of the diversity within a workforce.

Reflection Questions:

1. How in touch are you with your personal biases?

2. Who do you consider to be part of your personal "in-group", and who do you believe is perceived as part of the "in-group" within your organization?

3. What steps is your organization currently taking to promote and contribute to a more inclusive working environment?

4. What efforts has your organization, or you personally, made to address personal biases and behaviors that hinder the development of genuine relationships among employees and contribute to a more inclusive work environment?

5. What are your organization's current engagement, absence, and turnover rates? Are you collecting both qualitative and quantitative data to gain a comprehensive understanding of the current situation? Have you noticed any patterns or trends among specific employee demographics?

6. What feedback have former employees provided with regard to the inclusivity within your organization, either through public forums or during exit interviews?

7. Does your organization currently possess, or is it willing to cultivate, qualities such as humility, empathy, effective communication, and a commitment to personal development in order to foster a successful diverse workplace?

HAPHAZARDLY CREATING INITIATIVES THAT WON'T WORK LONG-TERM

After exploring the typical traps of shallow, superficial diversity efforts and the high cost of exclusion, it is a natural reaction to want to identify solutions to rectify these issues.

While most DE&I professionals will recommend taking a "comprehensive approach" to diversity and inclusion that suggest the use of policies, programs, and practices to address exclusion and promote diversity at all levels of an organization, it is important to avoid another common mistake: investing significant time, money, and effort into initiatives that are unlikely to support long-term improvements in DE&I.

The executive team of the organization I worked for abroad was painfully aware of the inefficiencies resulting from pushback by employees who were hesitant to work outside of their cultural or linguistic comfort zones.

Environmental regulations were going to make a majority of their products obsolete in the coming years. However, during a critical period when the organization needed to work together, ideate, and innovate, employees continued to be more focused on maintaining the status quo of hierarchy, justifying the way things had been historically done, and demonstrated reluctance to embrace English as the primary language of communication in the workplace.

The executive team had tried to make clear that the behavior that got them to where they were would not continue to do so even in the next 5 years, but the message wasn't getting through.

In an effort to promote a more globally minded and inclusive workplace culture that would feel empowered to find creative solutions, the HR department was tasked with creating a one-day cultural transformation workshop that would be mandatory for all 12,000 employees.

The workshop kicked off with videos clarifying the vision, mission, and values of the organization, highlighting the importance of their participation as an organization in the global economy.

Participants were then put into groups with colleagues they may have never previously interacted with, from departments across the organization, to participate in several initial exercises that displayed the value of diverse perspectives in problem solving.

The remainder of the day was left for group discussions regarding the company values.

Employees were tasked with identifying how they resonate with the organization's core values both personally and professionally, how they felt they were being carried out within the current working culture, and how they intended to live the values in their current working environment moving forward to achieve a more positive and collaborative work environment.

Through the guided, open discussions, facilitators uncovered current challenges the employees were facing within the working culture and addressed any concerns or queries related to fostering an international environment.

So, by the time every employee had gone through that one-day workshop, they were all able to completely change their behaviors, and were singing Kumbaya working together in total harmony... right?

Unfortunately, it didn't work that way.

After each workshop, I interviewed participants to see how productive they felt the event had been.

While generally participants seemed to have a sense of relief, excitement for the future of the organization, and gratitude, the same type of feedback kept arising.

One participant said to me directly, "This workshop was fantastic, and it was nice to talk about issues openly, but what will it matter tomorrow? I'm going to go back to work, and my boss is still going to be an asshole."

Employees didn't trust that a single workshop would really change their colleagues' behavior, and they weren't wrong to doubt that either.

Now, that comment and similar attitudes across participants is not to imply that this workshop had no impact at all.

The alignment as to where the organization was headed and assurance all employees would have a place in that, even if that meant their role and responsibilities would shift, was critical to get employees remotivated and on track with the organizational goals.

However, the uncertainty that all colleagues would really start to live the values that were reinforced in the workshop and behave in a more productive manner after the event was an indication that the exercises had only just scratched the surface and uncovered more deep-seated issues within the working culture.

When I presented some of the initial feedback to HR and suggested that additional feedback should be collected and utilized in follow-up initiatives to reinforce the learnings, one of the HR business partners jumped in, stating "We cannot solve everyone's individual problems. It sounds like personal issues they need to take up with their leader."

The consensus between the rest of the group became, the workshop was comprehensive enough already and should have empowered individuals to change their behavior, regardless of the actions of others and despite there being no additional guidance on how to navigate the changing culture moving forward.

As a result, no further actions were taken to follow up with the event.

In that HR department's defense, they believed that they had successfully identified and diagnosed the cultural problems and had already invested an exorbitant amount of time and resources to "fix" them. Beyond that, the success of the workshop had become a measure of their performance, and acknowledging the necessity for further efforts beyond the allocated budget and timeframe might have given the impression that it was a failure.

Sharing my disappointment, one of the facilitators shed some light on the practices of the companies they engage with. She explained to me how most companies they work with spend large sums of money and resources on workshops like these merely as a formality. Doing so allows them to tick off the diversity, inclusion, and corporate culture box for the year. However, what struck me as alarming was that most organizational leaders they worked with had a genuine belief that a single-day seminar could somehow magically bring about a revolutionary transformation. The facilitator went on to explain to me how most organizations choose not to follow up after these types of initiatives, resulting in the eventual loss of any progress that may have been made. This recurring cycle is precisely what keeps them employed as facilitators and what makes the workshops they run indispensable.

Although the cultural transformation workshop at my old company did have an impact by bringing more awareness, alignment, and clarity as to the necessity for cross-cultural collaboration, the expectation that it could single-handedly change the organizational culture and make everyone more open minded and collaborative despite the existing language barriers, to one in which all employees could work together in perfect harmony to become more innovative was unrealistic.

I've observed countless Chief Diversity Officers and HR decision makers take swift and expensive action based on quick assessments that attempt to solve problems that relate to diversity, equity, and inclusion.

To resolve whatever DE&I issue is on the table, someone is assigned to spearhead an initiative to address the matter, and in some instances, using limited resources.

That individual typically looks to best practices or what other organizations have done, such as workshops, seminars, forming internal councils or groups to represent specific issues minority groups face or tying leadership bonuses to diversity and inclusion initiatives.

Although some of these actions and solutions may very well be viable ways to address DE&I within certain environments, they're often short-term and surface-level countermeasures that lack any meaningful accountability measures. Furthermore, they often remain applicable only in isolated cases or for select individuals within the organization, and at times, lack any sort of resonance or relevance to anyone within the company at all.

Swift action without consideration of the root cause of ongoing organizational challenges only addresses symptoms of larger problems.

Although these actions can provide a temporary feeling of progress or accomplishment, they offer little to no insights into the underlying issues that need to be addressed to drive lasting change.

They ultimately become busywork that offers little value beyond temporarily boosting morale or providing a superficial sense of progress.

"Don't program a rocket which will fail."

—Eric Ries

Eric Ries describes in his book, *The Lean Startup*, the reason why so many startups fail.

According to Ries, the majority of startups fail because they've based their products or solutions on the assumption that people are actually going to want and need them.

Entrepreneurs spend months, and, in worst cases, even years, building and perfecting solutions based solely on market research and strategy.

Their solutions have a whole lot of vision to them with a whole lot more untested assumption.

They disregard collecting input from prospective customers as to whether their solution was even remotely interesting to them and then spend what money they have on a grandiose launch, just to find out that their solution is not as well received as they initially had anticipated it to be.

Customers or users express their indifference through not purchasing the product or service, and the startup fails because it ran out of money.

This phenomenon is quite the same with corporate DE&I initiatives.

Decision makers may think they know their organization's challenges like the back of their hand, either based on their own experience in the working culture or through the arbitrary data collected in employee engagement surveys.

They use what they think they know to develop solutions in order to address those challenges, and if they are convincing enough to get buy-in and permission from the leadership team, they start rolling out their solutions through some type of campaign expecting everyone in the organization to jump on board.

While some initiatives may gain initial traction in the short run, most result in little to no change in the long term. When they're unable to show any substantial results, they're denied a budget in the future and are unable to carry on with any future DE&I efforts.

Rather than directly scaling expensive and ineffective initiatives solely based on assumptions and expecting to see results, corporate initiatives should consider a different approach.

The methodology in *The Lean Startup* recommends using a Build-Measure-Learn Feedback Loop to obtain initial feedback from, in our case of corporate DE&I initiatives, employees.

This approach involves continuously iterating and improving the initiative using rapid experimentation and feedback to drive innovation and create solutions that will be effective in the long term.

The methodology can be broken down into the following steps:

Step 1. Define the problem.

The first crucial step before embarking on any initiative is to clearly identify the underlying problem or opportunity.

This requires keen observation of the surrounding working environment, paying close attention to employee behaviors, needs, and pain points. Emerging patterns or trends are good indicators of potential problems or opportunities.

Once a potential problem or opportunity has been recognized, additional research must be conducted to validate its existence and severity. This involves engaging with employees through interviews, surveys, or another form of feedback collection to assess the significance of the problem and determine if they are actively seeking a solution.

By further identifying patterns, similarities, and differences among respondents, employees can be categorized into distinct segments based on common characteristics and needs. This segmentation process can then provide valuable insights for formulating a more clearly defined problem statement.

All insights gathered during the problem validation phase should be used to develop a single refined problem statement.

This foundational research ensures a clear understanding of the core issue at hand, enabling the development of a focused solution that effectively addresses the problem.

Step 2. Formulate a Hypothesis

The next step using Lean methodology is to start brainstorming potential solutions.

Consider using brainstorming techniques, design thinking principles, or other creative methods to come up with several innovative solutions. The goal is to encourage diverse thinking and explore multiple ideas or hypotheses for potential solutions.

The result should be a single defined hypothesis that clearly articulates how a specific intervention or solution can effectively address the identified DE&I problem that had been outlined in step 1.

Step 3. Identify Key Metrics

The subsequent step involves determining the key performance indicators, otherwise referred to as metrics, that will help you measure the progress and success of your goal that is tied to your hypothesis.

To begin, break down your goal into specific and measurable objectives. Then, search for indicators that are specific, quantifiable, and directly tied to your DE&I goal.

When selecting metrics, ensure they are available and reliable.

Consider any gaps in data collection and reporting processes and work towards enhancing data collection methods to ensure accurate and dependable measurements.

Step 4. Building the Minimum Viable Product

Once a clear problem/opportunity, a well-defined hypothesis with the most promising intervention, and specific key performance indicators are established, you are finally ready to construct a minimum viable product (MVP).

A Minimum Viable Product is an inexpensive and basic version of a solution that can be developed and tested quickly. Its primary purpose is to serve as a tool for controlled experiments to enable the testing of assumptions and ongoing validation of the solution's demand.

To proceed, create a small-scale initiative or pilot program that encompasses the essential elements of your DE&I solution.

This is where solutions such as targeted training sessions, mentorship programs, or employee resource groups focused on specific underrepresented minorities are really put to the test.

Step 5. Test and Gather Feedback

After the development of the Minimum Viable Product, it is time to start rapidly testing it using the quantifiable metrics previously defined to determine its success or failure.

During and after implementation, it is essential to gather feedback from participants since they are the key stakeholders. Observation, surveys, interviews, and focus groups can be used to gain insights regarding their experiences and suggestions for improvement. This feedback will provide valuable insights on how to iterate and refine your approach. It also enables a deeper understanding of the solution's effectiveness.

To ensure accurate measurement of effectiveness, it is essential to ask critical questions and diligently track true and honest answers during testing. Observing how employees genuinely respond to the potential solution and collecting relevant data allows for informed decisions on whether to pivot to an alternative solution or further develop the initial idea.

Conducting thorough investigations into the solution's effectiveness will yield valuable insights and enable the development of better solutions before making any full-scale commitment to implementation.

Step 6. Measure and analyze results

After all the necessary data has been collected from the initial test, it is time to review the metrics established in the previous step and evaluate the impact of your MVP.

Evaluate whether the intervention has successfully achieved the desired outcomes in terms of diversity, equity, or inclusion.

This evaluation process also involves examining the validity of your initial hypothesis and determining its accuracy based on the observed results.

Step 7. Learn and pivot

Based on the insights gained from testing and analysis, decide whether to pivot, persevere, or iterate on your DE&I initiative.

A pivot involves making a significant change in your strategy, product direction, or segment you are targeting based on feedback and insights gained from testing and experimentation. This does not imply failure but is rather a strategic shift in response to discovering that the solution tested was not delivering the desired results. A pivot provides opportunity to explore alternative paths that have the potential to more effectively align with employee needs.

Perseverance refers to the decision to continue executing the existing strategy or MVP without making any significant changes. It involves staying the course and maintaining confidence in the current approach as a result of the feedback and data suggesting that the MVP or strategy is on the right track and delivering actual value to employees. Perseverance is appropriate when there is evidence of positive traction and validation of the assumptions and hypothesis.

Iteration is the process of making incremental changes or improvements to the MVP or solution based on feedback and data gathered during testing and experimentation. Iteration involves continuously refining and optimizing the solution to enhance its value, address identified issues, and align better with employee needs. The focus becomes learning from each iteration and making incremental adjustments to improve effectiveness for employees.

This step is completely dependent on the feedback and results from experimentation, it might involve adjusting your hypothesis if it was proven to be false, changing your approach altogether, or expanding the initiative to a larger scale.

Step 8. Scale and deploy

Once the effectiveness of a solution has been confirmed through the outlined iterative process, it is finally time to proceed with scaling it across the entire organization.

Create a plan to implement the refined solution and closely monitor its impact, ensuring that feedback is continually collected, and necessary adjustments are made accordingly.

Step 9. Foster continuous improvement

Foster a mentality of continuous learning and improvement by regularly reviewing and updating your DE&I initiative based on new insights, evolving circumstances, and emerging best practices.

Employee feedback must remain a primary consideration in all decision-making processes. This requires establishing an ongoing feedback loop that includes open discussions with employees to evaluate the effectiveness of the solution that is continuously being tested.

Now, you might be a bit skeptical and think to yourself that this type of experimentation seems complicated and time-consuming, particularly if you are under pressure to deliver immediate results.

However, I can assure you that these experiments can be conducted within a matter of weeks, without incurring exorbitant costs, and are actually crucial for achieving any sort of significant long-term progress.

Despite the testing and iterations involved in the process, it still takes only a fraction of the time and resources typically spent on traditional strategic planning and can in fact be done concurrently with strategic planning to better inform overall strategy.

This process not only provides a deeper understanding of the actual challenges and pain points faced by employees within the current workforce but also uncovers superior solutions that contribute to lasting change.

By involving key stakeholders and employees early on, you ensure that solutions are effective and well-aligned with their actual needs.

This strategy transforms uncertainties, assumptions, and risks into tangible knowledge or "sure things" that will guide your organization towards actual progress.

In the case of the one-day workshop, the organization I worked for could have saved a significant amount of time and money using Reis's methodology and achieved more satisfactory results.

Here's how:

Step 1. Define the Problem

The organization was undoubtedly under tremendous pressure to change their behavior, foster collaboration, and drive innovation. However, due to insufficient time spent on comprehensively observing and understanding the underlying problems within the working culture, the primary focus became addressing multiple large surface-level symptoms caused by much deeper issues.

Had they invested additional time in clearly identifying the core problem they needed to solve, they likely would have achieved a more desirable outcome.

Step 2. Formulate a Hypothesis

Due to the absence of a single, well-defined problem statement, the organization came up with a broad hypothesis that a comprehensive cultural transformation would be necessary to attain their desired goals of fostering a more global mindset, enhancing inclusion, and ultimately seeing greater innovation.

Consequently, they decided to implement the single-day transformational workshop as their chosen solution.

The hypothesis was overly general and lacked a clear articulation as to how the single-day workshop would effectively achieve a long-term cultural transformation.

Step 3. Identify Key Metrics

Without a hypothesis to break down and measure, the HR department of the organization was primarily being held accountable for completion metrics.

Instead of prematurely scaling the solution and then tracking completion rates, a more effective approach would have involved clearly defining and breaking down the workshop's objectives, and then aligning them with key performance indicators to test the hypothesis and determine effectiveness.

The selected metrics should have been more precise, measurable, and directly tied to the overall goal, enabling a more accurate evaluation of progress.

Step 4. Building the Minimum Viable Product

The organization opted to recruit professional facilitators from around the globe to create and conduct a handful of pilot programs for the workshop before expanding.

A more effective approach would have been to utilize more in-house talent who possessed a deep understanding of the prevailing challenges within the working culture for the initial pilot development and testing. Additionally, it would have been beneficial to treat the pilot programs as genuine experiments rather than prematurely assuming they needed to be professionally crafted comprehensive solutions.

This alternative method could have resulted in significant cost savings for the organization while maintaining the opportunity for more valuable feedback and improvement to the program before scaling up.

Step 5. Test and Gather Feedback

Rather than relying primarily on participant satisfaction responses from a limited number of pilot programs, a more advantageous approach would have involved conducting a higher number of comprehensive initial tests.

Furthermore, the evaluation of the initial pilot programs overlooked the assessment of employee behavior, engagement, and overall job satisfaction metrics following their participation. To ensure a more robust evaluation, it would have been beneficial to collect additional data and feedback during several more pilot programs while carefully reviewing previously identified KPI's. This approach would have provided valuable insights for assessing the validity of the hypothesis and identifying areas for potential improvements.

Additionally, close observation of participant behavior could have yielded valuable insights into the workshop's effectiveness. By making the following observations, the impact of the workshop could have been assessed:

a) Did employees demonstrate the desired behaviors and fully embrace the organizational values, even in challenging work environments?

b) Did participants exhibit increased levels of innovation and collaboration after completing the workshop?

c) To what extent did participants apply the strategies or principles they learned during the workshop?

d) Did participants actively recommend the workshop to colleagues whom they believed would benefit from it?

These observations would have offered valuable insights into the workshop's effectiveness, its influence on participant behavior, and its overall impact on the organizational culture.

Step 6. Measure and analyze results

Because the identified metrics did not accurately reflect the success or overall impact on the company culture of the initiative, the effectiveness of the workshop remained intangible and unclear.

Step 7. Learn and pivot

Due to inadequate analysis and a lack of reliable metrics to ascertain success, there was never a constructive discussion as to whether the organization should pivot, persevere, or iterate their initial solution.

If early observations had revealed that none of the initial participants demonstrated any changes in behavior, improved collaboration, or increased innovation, it would have been a clear indication of a flaw in the solution strategy. At that juncture, it would have been wise to either further develop the solution or explore an entirely new approach to better address the genuine needs of employees.

This proactive course of action would have ensured a more effective and tailored solution that aligns with the evolving dynamics of the workforce.

Step 8. Scale and deploy

Only after the effectiveness of the one-day workshop had been confirmed through a more iterative process, would it have finally been time to proceed with scaling it across the entire organization.

This would have saved the company a significant amount of money in the long run, enabling them to scale a solution that would have been far more effected to achieving their desired outcome.

Step 9. Foster continuous improvement

Feedback received after the pilot programs was not adequately considered, and the solution was scaled without thorough evaluation of its ongoing effectiveness.

By embracing a continuous measurement and iteration approach during the scaling of the initiative, it would have been possible to address employee concerns effectively and derive significant value. This iterative process would have facilitated the collection of additional feedback and data, leading to a more accurate assessment of the overall effectiveness of the solution.

This approach could have been instrumental in identifying underlying issues, uncovering opportunities for improvement, and ultimately enhancing the solution's effectiveness.

I provide this explanation not to berate my previous employer, but rather to underscore the costs and inefficiencies that can arise when DE&I initiatives are implemented in a haphazard manner.

By adopting a strategic and systematic approach akin to the principles of the Lean methodology, organizations can avoid unnecessary expenses and drive more effective and sustainable progress towards diversity, equity, and inclusion.

Main Takeaways:

- While it's important to be proactive and solution-oriented, rushing to scale solutions to diversity, equity, and inclusion challenges without proper planning and testing can actually be counterproductive.

- This can result in exorbitant amounts of wasted time, money, and effort on initiatives that will either miss the mark completely or not really lead to any long-term sustainable change.

- Using the principles from *The Lean Startup* will provide the tools necessary to test assumptions and vision of solutions before investing large sums of money in activities that aren't likely to work.

- The build-measure-learn feedback loop, inspired by *The Lean Startup* methodology, provides organizations with an opportunity to develop and test solutions faster and cheaper. By challenging the need for significant investment upfront, this iterative approach allows organizations to assess whether a solution is worth pursuing before committing substantial resources to it and scaling.

- Using Lean methodology can save time and money in the long run, while also ensuring that solutions address actual needs, are effective, and lead to meaningful progress in DE&I.

- By taking a more calculated and scientific approach, organizations can make more informed decisions and avoid costly busywork.

Reflection Questions:

1. What are the ongoing diversity, equity, and inclusion (DE&I) initiatives implemented within your organization? Do you feel like they are effective and address the current needs of employees within your organization?

2. Does your organization follow a systematic and data-driven approach to develop initiatives, or do decisions tend to be made more haphazardly?

3. Are there well-defined Key Performance Indicators (KPIs) used to measure the success of these initiatives?

4. Does your organization seek out and utilize employee feedback to iterate, pivot, or persevere with the implementation of their initiatives?

IMBALANCED ACCOUNTABILITY AND RESPONSIBILITY FOR DE&I

I'm tired of this company's political bullshit!

I actually said those exact words directly to the head of HR and my supervisor as I was politely being let go from the organization I had been fighting to change for the past three years.

I had finally reached my breaking point and could no longer hide my anger and frustration that had built up over my time.

I had previously been naive to the experience of discrimination based on my nationality.

Any form of overt discrimination based on race or nationality that I had witnessed, which even remotely crossed a line in a professional setting before working overseas, had been met with disciplinary action almost immediately.

So, you might imagine that when I was introduced to colleagues who refused to work with me because of the extra effort it took to work with a foreigner, questions regarding my intelligence based on my outgoing personality and physical appearance, and assumptions directed toward me regarding my competence based on the perceived quality of education in the United States, I was in utter disbelief and frankly outraged that such behavior was still tolerated within a corporation in the twenty-first century.

After I had been phased out of my team due to the lack of productive collaboration, I had found myself in a very bad place in my career.

I felt devalued, underutilized, and degraded, but I had still been determined to do something about it.

My purpose became twofold: I intended to prevent anyone else from going through what I did, and to work toward changing the discriminatory attitudes and beliefs within the organization.

My plan was to use research and data to prove the business case for DE&I, get buy-in, and start working on initiatives that would make the company better for the underserved minority and the company as a whole.

I alone intended to solve the company's diversity and inclusion problems, even if it was the last thing I did.

I became so completely entrenched in my research that six months had gone by without my notice.

My days and nights were spent learning all that I could about corporate DE&I strategies, organizational culture, and bias. I interviewed as many different colleagues as I could from all over the organization to understand the company history, different perspectives on the current working culture, and opinions on corporate DE&I.

My final product was a thorough 96-page study which, altogether, artfully articulated the business case for DE&I and a realistic starting point for them to work from.

The piece addressed real company data, current trends, organizational culture, and case studies from inside and outside the organization to form a well-rounded linear argumentation.

It concluded with 10 behaviors for the company to adopt in order to become more inclusive and better utilize their current workforce to retain talent and organically attract more diversity in the future.

I found a few key stakeholders who were willing to listen to what I had to say and set up an hour and a half meeting with them to present my findings.

My presentation was just as long and thorough as my research.

I had already anticipated every single rebuttal I could imagine based on what I assumed my biggest critics would say and made sure there was no room for error or dispute.

When I was finally done talking, I quickly realized that I used nearly the entire time to talk at my audience.

While they had been undoubtedly impressed by the amount of effort I had put into the study, one colleague directly making the comment "Holy shit, that was a lot of work." they were otherwise speechless.

As I was reflecting on how I could have presented better, I finally realized the impossibility of trying to single handedly change the negative attitudes, beliefs, and behaviors of everyone else in the organization.

One of the major pitfalls organizations face in terms of DE&I is an imbalance in accountability and responsibility.

There is a big difference between accountability and responsibility.

Being responsible means having a duty or obligation to fulfill a role or carry out the tasks necessary for something to be achieved. When someone is responsible for something, they have the authority, capability, or duty to ensure its completion or success.

Accountability, however, goes beyond responsibility. It refers to being answerable or liable for the outcome or results of a task or initiative. When someone is accountable, not only are they responsible but will also be expected to answer to and explain or justify the results or outcome and accept any associated consequences.

In my situation, I not only held myself accountable for DE&I but also took responsibility for achieving the desired outcomes. However, it is common for DE&I advocates to bear the entire burden of driving change, which can result in feelings of resentment and impatience.

As the weight of this burden grows heavier, it is easy for DE&I advocates to develop an expectation for immediate adoption of their beliefs within the organization, rather than making genuine efforts to understand the perspectives and values of others.

This approach frequently leads to insufficient support, as it fails to garner the necessary buy-in and participation from individuals who would otherwise be willing and essential in fostering a more inclusive workplace.

Although I had tried to stay professional about the situation I was in, it became obvious that I was doing this work out of my own frustration with the organization.

I had run out of patience with the current corporate culture and was no longer willing to meet anyone where they were if they were too close-minded for my liking.

Rather than looking past how badly my colleagues had hurt me in order to try to understand their fears and then meet them where they were at, I had become as unempathetic as I felt they were to me.

Ever since I started doing this work, I have unintentionally intimidated several people who have assumed I was going to come at them looking for anything offensive or politically incorrect with what they said, or that I was going to put some type of woke spell on them.

I understand where this negative perception comes from, as there are certainly some individuals in the field who continue to approach DE&I issues in a confrontational manner, demanding that non minorities conform to their personal agendas.

That was very similar to my initial approach of trying to tell a company how to behave, until I realized how ineffective it was.

While the intentions behind those abrasive methods are good, they typically only make people feel uncomfortable, ashamed, or disengaged.

During my time in South Africa, I attended a yoga class with other professionals. After one of the sessions, one of the gentlemen in the class politely asked what I did for a living.

I told him that I work in the DE&I space (like all the other clued-up professionals were saying those days).

He chuckled nervously and told me that I should recruit his daughters since they had become so passionate about DE&I after studying the history of apartheid in school.

He described how determined they had been to challenge him on his biases and level of empathy towards marginalized groups, given his privilege as a straight White male.

He told me that after having been grilled so often by them, he now plans to introduce himself as the super straight, super sorry, super White guy.

I nearly spit out my drink laughing so hard.

He was, of course, kidding, although I believe that behind every joke, there's always a bit of truth.

I understand firsthand how abrasive, confrontational approaches to DE&I can evoke discomfort and unease among individuals who are perceived as privileged.

I found myself in a conversation with another professional who worked in DE&I, during which she spent most of the conversation highlighting how White women have contributed to the oppression of people of color throughout history rather than the current work either of us were doing. As you can imagine, for someone who sincerely despises any form of discrimination, I didn't have a great feeling in my stomach after that conversation nor did I feel inclined to speak with her further.

Progress cannot be achieved through the anger and resentment of one person, nor can anyone expect a positive reaction out of others when they come in hot without having taken the time to understand where the other people are coming from.

I learned the hard way how my strong emotions could hinder my ability to empathize with and communicate effectively with my colleagues when working toward a solution for greater inclusion.

Regardless of how many facts, what data, and how much research I had to back me up, I wasn't going to convince anyone to become as angry as I was and join me in the fight I was fighting; therefore, my diversity study didn't lead to any concrete outcomes.

Throughout my career, I've encountered several other consultants who had to stop working in DE&I because they burnt out.

They had become so disheartened and resentful with what they perceived as simply ignorance of others. Frustrated by the slow progress of organizations, not jumping on board with what they wanted or meeting their expectations, they eventually lost patience and gave up.

After I had calmed down a bit from my outburst about the company's tolerance of discrimination, my supervisor tried to console me. He reminded me of the strides Martin Luther King Jr. had made in his lifetime in the fight for equality, and pointed out how much progress still needs to be made in the world even today.

An individual can start a movement and take accountability, but it takes the collective effort of the entire organization and a whole lot of time to start to see any real change.

There is never instant gratification, and in most cases, there is no gratification at all when it comes to DE&I work.

Very seldom are there clear, direct, and instantaneous outcomes to DE&I initiatives where everyone in a company is finally able to effectively come together, get along flawlessly, and directly start producing better business outcomes.

The success and outcomes of DE&I work is very much dependent on other people's behavior over long periods of time.

Inclusive behavior and equality aren't anything that can simply be mandated because the only thing you can really control, regardless of what position you hold within your organization, is yourself.

It's a common human reaction to feel anger, hurt, or frustration when others aren't behaving in a productive or inclusive manner, but dwelling on these emotions isn't productive for anyone. These feelings can prevent us from actively listening, understanding others, and finding clarity.

Once I set my research and anger aside, and started working on myself, I was eventually able to come to the realization that I simply represented the change within the organization which was still something that was new and scary for my colleagues.

As young professionals, my colleagues feared becoming irrelevant without advanced English language skills. They were under immense pressure to continually showcase their skills and come up with innovative ideas to drive the company's success. Meanwhile, they were also grappling with the remnants of a toxic corporate culture that had treated them unfairly, potentially worse than they had treated me. This made it challenging for them to find their footing and make positive contributions to the organization while also healing from their own past experiences.

Through my participation in a positive intelligence program, I was eventually able to access my inner sage mode, which has enabled me to respond more productively in challenging situations.

I learned to take a step back and simply observe situations as opposed to judge or control them.

This gave me a far more objective perspective.

I also learned how to imagine my difficult colleagues as their inner child. Through this exercise, I was able to better imagine them as their truest selves and empathize with them.

And lastly, I learned how to anticipate my own personal saboteurs and how they might impact my behavior in my professional environment, regardless of anyone else's actions. (Chamine, 2016)

Now, I'm not saying that these practices make discrimination okay or that discrimination should be tolerated. Some individuals are actually just overtly racist, and there should be clear antidiscriminatory policies in place and repercussions for those discriminating against others.

However, a stronger sense of empathy helps you to better understand the actions of those around you and can help you have more control over your reactions in order to navigate difficult environments more effectively.

No matter what hurt or frustration you might be experiencing, I strongly encourage you to do some internal deep work so you don't go on a 6-month hiatus to create a solution to DE&I that's going to be ineffective and ultimately lead you to burnout.

I didn't explain all of this to say suck it up buttercup, but no matter how much pain you're in, you can't have any productive conversation about DE&I in anger and without empathy, expecting to get anywhere good.

If you are the one advocating for DE&I, take the necessary steps to get your head and heart in the right place so you can effectively communicate with and engage the entire organization, encouraging them to embrace shared responsibility for DE&I and collaboratively drive meaningful change.

Remember, creating an inclusive and equitable workplace requires collective effort. When everyone feels accountable and personally responsible for DE&I, it becomes an integral part of the company's DNA, leading to meaningful and sustainable change.

If you're not currently advocating for DE&I, it's time to step up and recognize your role and responsibility in driving this important effort.

Key Takeaways:

- There is a difference between accountability and responsibility, and it is ineffective to consider one person or even one team both accountable and responsible for DE&I.

- Productive DE&I is not going to be accomplished through the anger or resentment of one person: that's a recipe for pushback and burnout.

- Regardless of the current state of the organization or the reactions and attitudes towards DE&I within the environment, progress cannot be achieved by imposing personal agendas or attempting to induce feelings of shame or guilt. Such approaches will only alienate individuals, including those who may have initially been supportive of the cause.

- Although a single individual can start a movement, diversity, equity, and inclusion require the participation of all employees in the organization. Everyone needs to be responsible for facilitating change, especially when it comes to DE&I.

- Anyone advocating for DE&I should take the time to do the deep work necessary to better understand and empathize with others.

- Quieting our inner saboteurs can enhance our empathy and help us approach discussions about diversity, equity, and inclusion with an open mind and heart. This, in turn, enables us to actively listen to diverse perspectives, engage in honest and constructive dialogue, and provide support to empower all individuals to contribute to DE&I efforts.

- Although we can't force people to act in a certain way, we can make an effort to understand their perspectives, motivations, and behaviors. By doing so, we can identify more comprehensive and effective solutions for improving productivity and collaboration.

Reflection Questions:

1. Who bears accountability for DE&I within your organization, and who carries the responsibility? Remember: Accountability refers to the individual who is answerable for the outcomes and consequences of DE&I efforts, whether they are positive or negative. Responsibility pertains to the individuals who have a duty or obligation to fulfill and execute the necessary tasks and duties of DE&I.

2. Is DE&I predominantly mandated within your organization, or is it a collaborative effort that is co-created by all stakeholders within the organization?

3. Do you and even further, does every member within your organization, including leaders, HR personnel, and employees at all levels, possess a comprehensive understanding of how their actions, behaviors, and roles within the organization influence DE&I?

4. Does everyone within your organization feel personally responsible for contributing to an inclusive working environment?

CONCLUSION

I hope that this book has made you laugh out loud at least once, as well as shed light on some of the intricate and pressing challenges in diversity, equity, and inclusion work.

Beyond that, my wish is for you to feel inspired to adopt a more authentic approach to diversity and break free from the monotonous cycle of crafting superficial campaigns, issuing hollow public commitments to DE&I, and relying on a Ctrl+C, Ctrl+V approach to initiative creation. It's time to move beyond the pursuit of quick fixes for the sake of appearing more diverse for convenient PR moments. Instead, I hope you now can recognize the value of rolling up your sleeves and making a more long-term investment in endeavors that foster an environment where your existing workforce can thrive to their fullest potential and organically attract and retain greater diversity in the future.

My intention was to provide a greater understanding of the history of DE&I work and empower you to take a more proactive approach within your organization. Remember, it doesn't always require an awkward or embarrassing moment to realize the need for greater equality among your colleagues. Get to know your colleagues and keep finding ways to help them perform better in their roles. Let your expanded understanding of just how complex diversity really is, also inspire you to wholeheartedly find ways to celebrate their unique skills and perspectives.

Additionally, I hope you have come to recognize the immense cost of exclusion and understand that simply hiring more diverse individuals is not going to magically create a more collaborative environment that cranks out innovative ideas all day long. May you find the courage and humility to get out of your own way, be curious and learn how to best collaborate with those already around you, irrespective of the differences or challenges you may perceive. And may your actions serve as an inspiration to others, encouraging them to embark on a similar journey of growth and collaboration.

And the next time Jeff or Suzie, a few cubicles over, recommend some type of corporate DE&I initiative they read about Google trying, I can only hope that you won't simply go along with it, but instead encourage a process of experimentation to validate hypotheses and test the most effective solutions that have the potential to truly enhance your organization's diversity, equity, and inclusion.

But above all else, I hope you feel a sense of relief from the burdens you may have been carrying. If you've made it all the way to the end of this book, you were either thoroughly entertained by the scandalous and tantalizing stories I've shared, or you genuinely care about DE&I and are committed to making your company better. Take a moment to acknowledge your efforts and cut yourself some slack. Remember, you are just one person, and the journey towards creating a more inclusive workplace takes collective effort and shared responsibility.

DE&I is no longer just a nice-to-have initiative, but a business imperative that drives innovation, creativity, and competitiveness in a rapidly changing world. By avoiding the common DE&I pitfalls explained in this book, your organization will set itself apart and attain the enduring results necessary for fostering effective collaboration and innovation in the long run.

I strongly urge you to embark on your own personal journey of self-reflection and growth, in order to get your head and your heart in the right place to be effective with this work. This transformative process will call for humility, curiosity, and the courage to deeply explore your own experiences and perspectives, as well as those of others who may have stark differences from you.

I then encourage you to engage in honest and constructive conversations using the reflection questions in this book as a foundation, with your colleagues, leaders, and stakeholders to identify the DE&I challenges and opportunities in your organization. By capturing diverse perspectives, you can gain a deeper understanding of the systemic barriers and cultural norms that may be hindering DE&I progress and co-create solutions that are necessary to address actual challenges within the current working culture.

Finally, I invite you to join me on a journey towards creating inclusive working environments that value and leverage people's unique brilliance. I am on a mission to empower both individuals and organizations to unleash their full potential and drive meaningful progress in the realm of diversity, equity, and inclusion. Drawing from my extensive research, experience, and unwavering passion for DE&I, I am genuinely interested in understanding and working through the unique DE&I challenges and opportunities faced by you and your organization.

Imagine the possibilities that would emerge if every member of your organization felt empowered to express their authentic selves and contribute their unique thoughts and ideas.

Now imagine if every team was then able to harness the collective power of diverse viewpoints to forge groundbreaking solutions.

It's time to start laying the groundwork to transform into an audacious company that is not only able to withstand any trials that come along with our rapidly changing environment but thrives amidst them.

Did I miss a pitfall? Have a different experience? Drop me a line at workwithallisondavis@gmail.com. I look forward to connecting with you, hearing about your experiences with DE&I work, and supporting your journey to create a workplace where authenticity, diversity, and innovation converge, shaping a brighter future for all.

WORKS CITED

Inauthentic in DE&I Efforts

Mahdawi, A. (2016). "Rent-A-Minority." https://rentaminority.com/.

Kochhar, S. (2016). Millennials@Work: Perspectives on diversity & inclusion. https://instituteforpr.org/ millennialswork-perspectives-diversity-inclusion/.

Pinilla, M., & Hampole, N. (2020, October 7). Investors are committing to action on diversity. Now what?: Blog: Sustainable Business Network and Consultancy." *BSR*, https://www.bsr. org/en/our-insights/blog-view/investors-are-committing-to-action-on-diversity-now-what.

Nguyen, L., & Green, J. (2020, December 1). Nasdaq joins Goldman in corporate push for more diverse boards. *Bloomberg*. https://www.bloomberg.com/ news/articles/2020-12-01/nasdaq-plans-to-require-more-diversity-on-listed-company-boards.

Hood, D. (2023, April 7). Lawsuits challenge corporate diversity pledges after Floyd. *Bloomberg Law*.

https://news.bloomberglaw.com/esg/host-of-companies-sued-alleging-unmet-diversity-equity-pledges?utm_medium=email&_hsmi=254841559&_hsenc=p2ANqtz-8LBBNJuTrE6R6MugX_KlSkezy-TPqNngwLM-F9F1eepDCQpM46o AG0YMM32uFNRSWNfuOW5YHcxxpqQ KfFlJ5IqhZgfEPhetHcFnDJEm5ifY43DFw&utm_content=254841559&utm_source=hs_email.

Caught in a Reactive Cycle Rather Than Taking a Proactive Approach to DE&I

Vaughn, B. E. (2018, June 17). The history of diversity training & its pioneers. *Diversity Officer Magazine.* https://diversityofficermagazine.com/diversity-inclusion/the-history-of-diversity-training-its-pioneers/.

Sleek, S. (2018, January 31). "The bias beneath: Two decades of measuring implicit associations." *Association for Psychological Science.* https://www.psychologicalscience.org/observer/the-bias-beneath-two-decades-of-measuring-implicit-associations.

The industry gender gap women and work in the Fourth Industrial Revolution. (2016). *World Economic Forum.* www3.weforum.org/docs/WEF_FOJ_Executive_Summary_GenderGap.pdf.

Leonard, B. (2018, April 11). Study suggests bias against "Black" names on resumes. *SHRM.* https://www.shrm.org/hr-today/news/hr-magazine/pages/0203hrnews2.aspx.

Study finds major discrimination against Turkish job applicants. (2010). *The Local* www. thelocal.de/20100209/25145.

Hudson, C. (2023, March 16). Wells Fargo ignored diversity problems, shareholders say in suit. *Bloomberg Law*. https://news.bloomberglaw. com/esg/wells-fargo-ignored-diversity-problems-shareholders-say-in-suit.

Limiting The Definition of Diversity to Superficial Features

Hunt, V., Yee, L., Prince, S., & Dixon-Fyle, S. (2018, January). Delivering through diversity. https://www.mckinsey.com/capabilities/ people-and-organizational-performance/ our-insights/delivering-through-diversity

Alliant International University. What are the 4 types of diversity in the workplace? https://www. alliant.edu/blog/what-are-4-types-diversity.

Not Including the Diversity that's Already Employed

Jana, T., & Freeman, M. (2016). *Overcoming bias: Building authentic relationships across differences*. Berrett-Koehler Publishers.

Nadal, K. L. (2018). *Microaggressions and traumatic stress: Theory, research, and clinical treatment*. American Psychological Association, 2018.

Hicken, M. T., Lee, H., Morenoff, J., House, J. S., & Williams, D. R. (2014). Racial/ethnic disparities in hypertension prevalence: Reconsidering the role of chronic stress. *American Journal of Public Health.* https://www.ncbi.nlm. nih.gov/pmc/articles/PMC3910029/.

White paper: Absenteeism - The bottom line killer. (2005). *CIRCADIAN® White Paper,* https:// www.circadian.com/white-paper-absenteeism.

The cost of replacing an employee and the role of financial wellness. (2016, January 15). https://www. enrich.org/blog/The-true-cost-of-employee-turnover-financial-wellness-enrich#:~:text=The%20 Society%20for%20Human%20Resource,in%20 recruiting%20and%20training%20costs.

Sweet, J., & Shook, E. (2020). Accenture getting to equal the hidden value of culture makers. https:// www.slideshare.net/accenture/culture-of-equality-in-the-workplace-accenture-229599385.

Diversity Study - Yello. https://yello.co/wp-content/ uploads/2018/10/TL_2018_Diversity_Study.pdf.

The true cost of absenteeism in the workplace and how gap cover can prevent it. (2022, August 3). *Fanewscoza RSS.* https://www.fanews.co.za/ article/employee-benefits/3/general/1221/ the-true-cost-of-absenteeism-in-the-workplace-and-how-gap-cover-can-prevent-it/35148.

Haphazardly Creating Initiatives
that Won't Work Long-term

Ries, E. (2017). *The lean startup: How today's
entrepreneurs use continuous innovation to create
radically successful businesses.* Currency.

Imbalanced Accountability and
Responsibility for DE&I

Chamine, S. (2016). *Positive intelligence: Why only 20% of
teams and individuals achieve their true potential and how
you can achieve yours.* Greenleaf Book Group Press.

AUTHOR BIO

Allison Davis is a dynamic and passionate young woman with a profound commitment to diversity, equity, and inclusion (DE&I). Her transformative experiences abroad and relentless pursuit of understanding DE&I dynamics have shaped her perspective and fueled her dedication to creating positive change.

During her time working abroad for an organization that purported to value diversity but fell short, Allison witnessed firsthand the detrimental effects of performative inclusivity. Motivated by this disillusionment, she resolved to dive deeper into the realm of DE&I, determined to uncover the truth and drive authentic transformation.

With a unique blend of academic and practical expertise, Allison has extensively researched DE&I for various organizations, shedding light on the importance of authentic DE&I efforts. Her studies have taken her to the most extreme cases in South Africa, providing her with a nuanced understanding of DE&I challenges within complex socio-political contexts.

Drawing from her personal encounters and rigorous research, Allison weaves together narratives, insights, and evidence-based strategies in her writings. She possesses a remarkable ability to bridge theory and practice, empowering individuals and organizations to confront their biases, foster genuine inclusivity, and cultivate lasting change.

As an emerging voice in the field of DE&I, Allison is committed to highlighting the compelling business case for diversity and inclusion while providing a thought-provoking and introspective outlook on the subject matter. Through her work she strives to inspire others to challenge the status quo, embrace diversity in all its forms, and build a more equitable workforce for future generations.

URGENT PLEA!

Thank You For Reading My Book!
I really appreciate all of your feedback and
I love hearing what you have to say.

I need your input to make the next version of this
book and my future books better.

Please take two minutes now to leave a helpful review on
Amazon letting me know what you thought of the book:

https://www.amazon.com/dp/B0CD15L67Z

Thanks so much!

- Allison Davis

Made in the USA
Coppell, TX
20 September 2023